Risk Based Auditing:

Using ISO 19011:2018

CERM Academy Series on

Enterprise Risk Management

Greg Hutchins PE CERM
CERMAcademy.com
QualityPlusEngineering.com
503.233.1012
800.COMPETE

HOW TO ORDER:

Cost is $69.00 per copy plus $6.00 Shipping/Handling in U.S. Offshore orders are based on the form of delivery. Quantity discounts are available from the publisher.

Quality Plus Engineering 503.233.1012
4052 NE Couch St. 800.COMPETE
Portland, OR 97232 800.266.7383
USA GregH@CERMAcademy.com

For bulk purchases, on company letterhead please include information concerning the intended use of the books and the number of books to purchase.

TABLE OF CONTENTS

PREFACE

This book is called **Risk Based Auditing**. The book is based on ISO 19011:2018, which are Guidelines for Managing Management Systems.

ISO 19011:2018 FORWARD

ISO is an acronym for the International Organization for Standardization. ISO is a worldwide group of national standards organization. These national standards associations are called ISO member bodies.

International standards are developed through ISO Technical Committees. ISO Technical Committee TC 176, for example, develops ISO 9001:2015 standard. ISO TC 262 develops the international risk management standard, ISO 31000.

The U.S. member body associated with ISO is the American National Standards Institute (ANSI). Each national standards organization can establish or be a member of an ISO Technical Committee. The national standard bodies send representatives to the Technical Committee to develop standards in a particular area. The Technical Committee may have members from many countries developing a standard that interests the particular national bodies.

International organizations, non-governmental organizations, government organizations, and private organizations can participate in an ISO Technical Committee. For example, ISO works with the International Electrotechnical Commission (IEC). Electric technical issues impact every country. For example, every electrical product or consumer electronics product or software product can be impacted by ISO and IEC directives. ISO has developed different approval criteria for standards development based on different types of ISO standards.

While ISO intends to develop generic and universally applicable standards and documents, there is a possibility that some parts of a standard may have intellectual property rights belonging to a company or audit organization.

ISO standards and guidelines go through many revisions and are vetted by global experts in the specific subject. However, common terms which may be protected in one country sometimes may be incorporated into the standard. ISO warrants that is not responsible for identifying such an Intellectual Property rights. ISO maintains good faith efforts that any patent or intellectual property rights are removed from the document or identified during the development of the standard. In the meantime, ISO is not responsible for the use or infringement of these rights.

ISO uses terms which may be trademarked in the standard. ISO maintains that it does not provide testimonial of the trademark.

ISO standards are largely voluntary. They are intended to promote the free movement of products and services. The meaning of ISO specific terms, processes, and expressions that are related to the standard or to conformity assessment adhere to the World Trade Organization (WTO) principles related to open trade.

ISO 19011: 2018 was prepared by the project committee ISO 302, Guidelines for Auditing Management Systems.

ISO 19011:2018 is the third edition of the standard.

The current standard can be used in place of the previous standard developed in 2011.

19011:2018 is a significant update from the previous standard. The main differences between the prior standard and the current revision are:

- Addition of risk based auditing.
- Addition of risk based principles to auditing.
- Expansion on the guidance for managing a Management System audit.
- Inclusion of risk in developing the management of an audit program.
- Guidance for conducting an audit, especially planning the audit.
- Clarification on the generic auditor requirements.
- Review and changes in the use of audit technology and process terminology.
- Removal of the appendix listing competence requirements for auditing of specific ISO Management System standards.
- Additional informative (optional) guidance.

Currently, more standards and guidelines are being developed in different Management System disciplines so it would be difficult to list all of the specific requirements required to conduct individual Management System audits.

Annex A in the back of ISO 19011:2018 provides guidance on conducting an audit as well as clarifies such concepts as organizational context, virtual audits, compliance, supply chain audits, and leadership commitment.

Commentary: ISO 19011:2018 is a major rewrite. The standard impacts all ISO certified companies, Certification Bodies, consultants, and ultimately clients relying on the certification assurance.

INTRODUCTION

The second edition of ISO 19011 was published in 2011. Since 2011, new Management System standards have been developed and published. These new standards follow a structure commonly referred to Annex SL. As well, many of the new standards have identical numbering and structure. Common terms and definitions are used in these new standards.

NEW AUDITING REQUIREMENTS

A broader approach to Management System auditing is now required incorporating risk, context, and new requirements. The guidance and direction for conducting Management System audits are now more specific.

Management System audits are now used by interested parties. Audit results are shared with multiple stakeholders, clients, and interest parties. Audit results can provide information for general business planning, risk-controls, and identify opportunities for improvement within the organization.

ISO 19011:2018 can also be used in other ways. It can be used to evaluate single or multiple audit criteria, which may include:

- Requirements ('shalls') identified in a Management System standard.
- Performance requirements identified in a policy or procedure.
- Compliance requirements identified in a statute, rule or specification.

- Risk requirements specified in a statute, rule, or organizational directive.
- Business or Management System objectives that must be achieved.
- Policies and procedures that must be followed by auditors.
- Statutory and regulatory requirements.
- Management System processes required by the organization or audit parties.
- Management System requirements in plans required by the organization or audit parties.

Commentary: ISO 19011:2018 uses different words for its audit phases. We use the following convention throughout this book of: 1. Planning the audit; 2. Conducting the audit; and 2. Reporting the audit.

ISO 19011:2018

ISO 19011:2018 is a generic document that provides auditing guidance for all types, sizes, and elements of an organization. To use the guidance offered in ISO 19011:2018, an audit must be scaled and tailored to the intent, requirements, complexity, type, scope, assurance level, and scale of the assessment.

ISO 19011:2018 offers guidance that can be tailored to the context of the organization including intent, requirements, complexity, type, scope, assurance level, and scale of the audit project.

ISO 19011: 2018 can be used for first-party, second-party, and third-party audits. First-party audits are internal audits within the organization. Second-party audits relate to the supplier or audit organization close to an end-product manufacturer. Third-party audits are independent and objective audits conducted by an audit organization on related to the client of the audit or the party being audited.

The size and composition of the audit team is determined by the intent, nature, and context of the audit. For example, a complex audit of a large organization could entail a large audit team while an audit of a smaller organization could be conducted by a single person.

Commentary: ISO 19011:2018 must be designed to the auditee's context. This is one of the powerful and consistent messages in the standard.

ISO 19011:2018 CONVENTIONS

ISO 19011:2018 relies on several conventions to make it readable and applicable. For example, the standard can be applied to multiple Management Systems. As well, the standard refers to individual auditor and is applicable to multiple auditors in a team.

ISO 19011:2018 intended users of the standard include a number of stakeholders. Users of the standard may include: auditors; organizations certifying to a or multiple Management System; clients auditing suppliers; internal auditors; regulatory auditors; contractual auditors; compliance auditors; interested parties, and audit clients. It is noted that the guidelines can be adapted and tailored to the needs of the organization and different parties.

So 19011:2018 can be used by organizations that want to self-declare compliance to a Management System standard. The document can be used for Management System auditor training and personnel certification of auditors.

ISO 19011:2018 is a guidance document. Its primary goal is to be flexible so that it can be used by different organizations in different contexts in different parts of the world. However, it should be noted that ISO 19011:2018 must be tailored to the audit objectives, complexity, size, intent, scope, and maturity level of the organization's Management System.

More companies are adopting an integrated Management System approach to their Management System certification. As a result, ISO 19011:2018 can be used in a combined audit approach where two or more Management Systems can be audited simultaneously. This is called an integrated audit approach. In this approach, different Management Systems are integrated into a single Management System so the principles and processes of planning, conducting, and reporting the audit are similar in the combined audit approach.

ISO 19011:2018 provides guidance to the management of the audit program including planning, conducting, and reporting by the Management System auditor.

ISO 19011:2018 also describes the knowledge, skills, and abilities of the auditors and audit team .

Commentary: ISO 19011:2018 will be used by ALL internal Management System auditors to audit ALL Management System Standards. ISO 19011:2018 will be used by ALL Certification Bodies when auditing companies.

GUIDELINES FOR AUDITING MANAGEMENT SYSTEMS

1. SCOPE

ISO 19011:2018 is a guidance document on auditing ISO Management System standards. The document provides guidance on:

- Principles of auditing Management Systems.
- Managing the audit program.
- Planning the Management System audit.
- Conducting the audit.
- Reporting the audit findings.
- Auditor requirements.

As well, ISO 19011:2018 can be used for determining and evaluating the competence of the individuals conducting audits. The critical people for conducting audits include the audit program manager, audit team lead, individual auditors, technical experts, and audit observers.

ISO 19011:2018 can be used by all organizations that need to plan, conduct, and report internal or external audits of Management Systems and managing an audit program. The guidelines can be used for certification of Quality Management System, Environmental Management System or any existing Management System or one currently in development.

As well, the guideline can be used for audit types of audits and types of assurance.

2. NORMATIVE REFERENCES

There are no normative references in ISO 19011:2018.

3. TERMS AND DEFINITIONS

ISO 19011:2018 has the number of specific auditing terms and definitions.

ISO and IEC have standardized auditing terms and definitions that are covered in this section.

3.1 AUDIT

Auditing is an independent, objective, and linear process for obtaining evidence to determine whether audit criteria or objectives have been met.

There are two Notes to this definition. Note one states that internal audits are called first-party audits. First-party audits are conducted by audit professionals on behalf of the internal organization requesting the audit.

Note two states that external audits of an organization are second-party and third-party audits. The second-party audit is conducted by organizations or clients of an associated company, such as an end-product manufacturer requesting a supplier audit. Third-party audits are conducted by an independent organization such as a registrar or Certification Body (CB) to determine compliance of a Management System standard. A third-party audit may also be conducted to determine statutory compliance or effectiveness of its Management System.

3.2 COMBINED AUDIT

Combined audit is conducted by an auditor of two or more Management Systems or compliance activities.

There is one Note to this definition. Note one states that ISO Annex SL is standardizing the structure of all Management System standards. This allows for more streamlined interpretation, design, and deployment of a Management System. These are known as Integrated Management Systems. An audit team can now audit two or more different Management Systems in one visit.

3.3 JOINT AUDIT

Joint audit is conducted of a single organization, commonly called a single audit by two or more auditing organizations. For example, two different clients may audit a common supplier jointly. Each wants an independent appraisal of the supplier's abilities to deliver consistent products or quality services. Or, two different clients may want to evaluate different elements of the supplier's capabilities.

3.4 AUDIT PROGRAM

Audit program is the structure and activities to plan, conduct, and report an audit. Audit program specifically determines scope, time frame, requirements, and costs to ensure that client requirements can be and are being met.

3.5 AUDIT SCOPE

Audit scope is the extent, depth, conditions, resources, and boundaries of an audit.

There are two Notes to the definition. Note one includes all the critical elements to ensure the audit can be conducted in a timely and cost-effective manner. Audit scope at a minimum may include: physical location of the audit; virtual location (cloud, offsite, etc.) of the audit; functions audited; organizational units audited; activities audited; processes evaluated; products reviewed; transactions checked; projects reviewed; programs reviewed and other audit elements. As well, audits are time and cost constrained.

Note two describes where the auditee is located. Location can be real or virtual. The real location of the auditee is where the company, business unit, and plant are located. A virtual location such as the cloud is where the auditee conducts most of its work, services, manufacturing, or design thus allowing the audit team to plan, conduct, and report the audit on time.

3.6 AUDIT PLAN

Audit plan is a narrative of the step-by-step activities that are needed to plan, conduct, and report the audit.

3.7 AUDIT CRITERIA

Audit criteria consist of the set of specific requirements that the auditor evaluates to determine audit adherence, compliance, effectiveness, efficiency, and economics. Objective evidence is gathered to determine whether these criteria and requirements have been adequately and suitably met.

There are two Notes to this definition. Note one states that audit criteria may consist of legal, statutory, regulatory, rules, or policy requirements. Concepts such as compliance or non-compliance are used in an audit finding which is the result of the audit. Compliance or non-compliance are binary terms meaning that audit criteria have been met or have not been met. If audit criteria have not been met in a compliance audit, then auditor issues a noncompliance finding.

Note two states audit criteria may include policies, procedures, work instructions, contractual requirements, legal requirements, and other critical audit elements.

3.8 OBJECTIVE EVIDENCE

Objective evidence consists of artifacts that support the existence, suitability, adequacy, validity, accuracy, or reliability of a requirement. Objective evidence is used to support the finding of an audit. Objective evidence is the basis of the audit trail leading to a finding.

There are two notes with this definition. Note one states that objective evidence can be obtained through analysis, observation, interviews, testing, and by other audit methods.

Note two states that objective evidence is used to determine, verify, and validate audit criteria or audit requirements.

3.9 AUDIT EVIDENCE

Audit evidence consists of information, records, data, statements from interviewees or audit information that can be used to determine whether there is adherence to audit criteria. Audit evidence can be verifiable and valid.

3.10 AUDIT FINDINGS

Audit findings are the outcomes or results of the audit. The auditor obtains sufficient audit evidence and evaluates adherence against audit criteria.

There are three notes to this definition. Note one states that audit findings may indicate conformity or non-conformity based on the audit requirements and criteria.

Note two states that audit findings can lead to the identification of risks both upside (opportunity) risk and downside (consequence) risks. These audit findings can be reported as opportunities for improvement if there are upside risks.

Note 3 states if audit criteria, requirements, or objectives are statutory or regulatory, then the audit finding is expressed as compliance or non-compliance to meeting the statutory requirement.

3.11 AUDIT CONCLUSION

Audit conclusion is the termination of the audit. Audit conclusion is determined when audit findings have been written, final report has been delivered to the audit client, closing conference with the auditee has been conducted, and final audit work papers are collected.

3.12 AUDIT CLIENT

Audit client is the same as audit client. The audit client is the organization or person that has requested and has authorized an audit.

There is one note to this definition. if an internal audit is being conducted, the audit client is the auditee or the organization managing and planning the audit program. For an external audit, the audit client can be regulators, end-product manufacturers, governmental organizations, nongovernmental organizations, or other audit clients.

3.13 AUDITEE

The auditee is the organization or person that is being audited. The following at the auditee may be audited: organization, area, plant, transaction, product, process, project, or even transactions.

3.14 AUDIT TEAM

Audit team can be one person or multiple persons planning, conducting, and reporting the audit. The audit team can be supported by technical experts and advisors.

There are two notes to this definition. Note one states that a multiple person on a team will have an audit team lead. This person is responsible for planning, conducting, and reporting audit results. This person has the authority and responsibility for ensuring audit requirements are being met.

Note two states that the audit team may include auditors in training and observers.

3.15 AUDITOR

The auditor is the person who plans, conducts, and reports the audit results. Auditor can be a single person or be part of a team in a large audit.

3.16 TECHNICAL EXPERT

Technical expert is the person who provides specific knowledge, and skills, where the person's abilities are required to plan, conduct, and report the audit. Technical expert may or may not be part of the audit team.

There are two notes this definition. Note one states that specific knowledge, skills, or abilities may be required to plan, conduct and report the audit. Technical expert may provide the audit team with technical assistance relating to the organization, person, activity, process, product, project, service, program, technology, and area being audited.

Note two states that the technical expert in the audit team may or may not serve as an auditor.

3.17 OBSERVER

The observer is a person who observes the planning, conducting, or reporting by the audit team. The observer does not act or serve as an auditor.

3.18 MANAGEMENT SYSTEM

Management System consists of interrelated and interacting organizational elements that are designed to produce a desired outcome or result. Management System may consist of policies, objectives, and processes that are designed and deployed to achieve specific objectives.

There are three notes to this definition. Note one states the Management System can consist of a single or multiple knowledge domains or areas. For example, a Management System may include a Quality Management System such as ISO 9001 2015, or Environmental Management System such as ISO 14001:2015.

Note two states that Management System elements consist of an organization's structure, authorities, roles, responsibilities, planning, policies, practices, beliefs, objectives, and processes to ensure that these objectives can be achieved.

Note three states that the scope of the Management System can include the entire enterprise, program, projects, processes, transactions, or products. The scope can include multiple functions within the organization or be limited to a single area to be evaluated.

3.19 RISK

Risk is the effect of uncertainty on the Management System or business objective. Some ISO standards refer to risk as the effect of uncertainty on objectives. There are four notes to this definition.

Note one states that an effect can be variation from the required objective or around an expected outcome, which can be either positive or negative.

Note two refers to uncertainty resulting from lack of data or information as a result from not understanding an event specifically its consequences or likelihood.

Note three states that risk is defined in terms of an event and its possible consequences.

Note four states that risk can be a combination of consequence or likelihood associated with an event occurring.

3.20 CONFORMITY

Conformity is the assurance of compliance to satisfy a requirement or the result of meeting a requirement. Conformity is often a binary term, meaning that an auditee conforms or does not conform to a requirement which is often statutory or regulatory.

3.21 NONCONFORMITY

Nonconformity is the opposite of conformity. Nonconformity is the inability to satisfy or meet a requirement. Requirements may involve an audit objective or a regulatory requirement.

3.22 COMPETENCE

Competence is the ability to confirm that a person has the requisite knowledge, skills, and abilities to conduct his or her work in a professional manner. Auditing often has specific requirements to demonstrate competence. Concept such as due professional care is often used to demonstrate that an auditor has the requisite competence.

Commentary: Incorporate these definitions into your Management System audit plans. These definitions ensure everyone is speaking the same auditing language.

3.23 REQUIREMENT

Requirement is an expectation, need, or requisite objective that is stated as an audit objective. The requirement or normally requirements define the purpose of an audit. Interestingly, ISO states that a requirement can be implied or obligatory.

There are two notes to this definition. Note one states that generally implied refers to a common practice within the organization that would be considered a common or good practice. Generally implied states that the need or expectation is generally understood. Generally implied can be the way an organization conducts its business.

Note two states that a specified requirement is defined in the scope of the audit and must be fulfilled.

3.24 PROCESS

Process is a series of tasks or activities that produce an outcome. A process usually has inputs, repeatable steps, and an outcome or result.

3.25 PERFORMANCE

Performance is the outcome that can be measured based on effectiveness, efficiency, and economics. There are audit performance measures that are used such as suitability, accuracy, and reliability in audits.

There are two notes to this definition. Note one states that performance can either be quantitative or qualitative.

Note two states that performance may refer to enterprise, programmatic, project, service, products, or service activities.

3.26 EFFECTIVENESS

Effectiveness is the manner in which audit tasks are completed and outcomes are achieved.

Commentary: ISO 19011:2018 auditing definitions are derived from ISO 9000:2015. The definitions are largely consistent with ISO 31000:2018, ISO 9001:2015, and other Management System standards. This is the one of the critical goals of Annex SL, which is ISO's goal to harmonize definitions, principles, and processes in various ISO standards and guidelines.

ISO 19011:2018 may be used in a larger organizational context. For example, the audit organization, audit client, and auditee may be using diverse risk frameworks and audit standards.

Commentary: The appendix to this book has a glossary of risk and audit terms, that can assist the auditor in understanding diverse audit standards and risk guidelines.

4.0 PRINCIPLES OF AUDITING

Auditing is based on a good management principles and good auditing practices. ISO causes good practices auditing principles. By following good auditing principles and practices, the audit team can:

- Ensure with a higher level of assurance, the audit will be effective, efficient, and economic.
- Ensure the audit becomes a value added, management tool.
- Ensure that management controls and policies are in place.
- Provide information to organizational stakeholders that management policies are being followed.
- Ensure Management System objectives can be and are being met.
- Ensure controls are being applied within the risk appetite of the organization.

Audit planning, conducting, and reporting should follow good auditing principles. The application of these principles ensures that audit results are understood and can be relied on by clients and interested parties of the audit report.

As well, audit results can be scalable and replicable. In other words, independent third parties would able to reach the same results by reading the audit report and following the auditor's logic trail.

ISO 19011:2018 offers seven principles of good auditing:

a. **Integrity**

Integrity is the quality of being transparent, honest, and being truthful. This is the core of any Management System audit.

Audit managers and auditors can:

- Conduct their work with high ethics, fairness, and truthfulness.
- Accept an audit assignment only if the audit organization is capable and proficient in being able to meet audit requirements and objectives.
- Plan, conduct, and report audit results in an objective and independent manner.
- Recognize, identify, and report any facts that may impair the independence of the auditor.

b. **Transparent presentation**

Transparent presentation means that audit findings, conclusions, recommendations, and results reflect the reality, facts and evidence of the audit. If there are any constraints or risks identified in the audit, they can be reported to the audit client. If there is a difference of opinion among team members or between the auditee and the audit team, they can be acknowledged in the final audit report.

Transparent and fair presentation of audit results imply a number of important attributes. The report can accurately describe the logic trail that led to each finding including audit criteria listed in an audit objective. The report is independent and objective. The report is honest in terms of being accurate and reliable. The report is sufficiently complete so that an independent third-party auditor would reach the same results as the audit team. The audit can focus on the Management System and processes as much as possible.

c. **Due professional care**

Due professional care is the application of professional care and the appropriate level of skill expected that a reasonably prudent and competent auditor would exercise in similar circumstances.

Auditors exercise due professional care when they conduct the audit based on a reliable audit plan, conduct the report in a reasonable manner, and report results in an objective and independent fashion.

Several ways to demonstrate due professional care include:

- Auditors are sufficiently trained to conduct the audit.
- Auditors agree that all audit objective and requirements have been met.
- Auditors are impartial and independent.
- Auditors follow a standard process and obtain sufficient evidence to reach their conclusions and findings.
- An independent third-party would reach the same conclusions as the auditors did.

d. **Confidentiality**

Confidentiality is ability to keep sensitive, secret, and personal information protected. Auditors exercise discretion in the use and protection of the auditee and client information during their audit. Often, auditors are requested to sign a nondisclosure or similar agreement prior to the audit.

Information gathered directly or indirectly as a result of the audit can be prioritized in terms of importance. Customer, client, or auditee audit information that is confidential, secret, and proprietary can be protected.

More information gathered in statutory audits are subject to regulations for maintaining records.

e. Independence

Independence is the condition where the auditor and audit team follow an objective approach to plan, conduct, and report audit results. Independence implies the auditor cannot be pressured, intimidated, or compromised in his or her ability to provide unbiased audit decisions.

Auditors can be unbiased and have no conflicts of interest. More often, implied and explicit conflicts of interest need to be disclosed. And, in both cases the auditor may have to recuse himself or herself from the audit.

Internal auditors, or first-party auditors can be independent from the area being audited. Implied or the appearance of conflicts of interest may compromise the audit.

All types of auditors, first-party, second-party, and third-party, should be objective in the planning, conducting, and reporting the audit in a professional manner.

Audit findings and conclusions can be based on reliable, suitable, and accurate audit evidence.

In smaller organizations, the Management System auditor may be the audit manager as well as the organization's first-party, second-party, and third-party auditor. The audit may not be fully independent of the function or area being audited. However, possible conflicts or even the appearance of conflicts should be fully disclosed to all audit stakeholders prior to the audit.

f. **Evidence based approach**

Evidence-based approach to auditing is intended to optimize risk based, decision-making in any type of audit. Evidence-based approach is a systematic and rational audit method for reaching accurate, suitable, and reliable audit findings and conclusions.

Audit evidence supports audit decisions and findings. Audit evidence is the basis of an audit trail. Audit evidence can be valid and verifiable. Audit evidence can be based on a reasonable approach.

Audit evidence can be qualitative or qualitative. Quantitative audit evidence is based on statistical analysis and samples gathered from a population of items. Qualitative audit evidence is gathered from interviews and analysis of documents.

Audits are time and resource constrained. So within the time frame of the audit, the audit team should collect sufficient evidence so that the team can develop reasonable assertions, conclusions, and findings.

An evidence-based approach is based on the risk appetite of the audit team and ultimate risk of the audit.

g. **Risk based approach**

Risk-based approach considers risks and opportunities in planning, conducting, and reporting the audit. The risk-based approach is relatively new concept in ISO 19011:2018. The risk-based approach considers risks and opportunities.

Risk-based approach implies that audits focuses on the significant risks for the audit client, auditor, and auditee help to ensure that audit objectives can be realized.

From the audit client's point of view, the client believes the accuracy and reliability of audit findings. From the auditor's point of view, a risk-based approach helps to ensure that audit requirements can be met. From the auditee's point of view, the audit will be fair and objective, so audit results can be used as the basis for improving operations.

Commentary: More ISO standards are structured around principles. ISO 19011:2018 is built around the above principles. An ISO certified organization or any organization focusing on operational excellence may want to build its Management System auditing program around the above principles.

5.0 MANAGING AN AUDIT PROGRAM

5.1 GENERAL

Audit program is the structure for managing, planning, conducting, and reporting an audit. The structure of an audit program is determined by the type, requirements, number, extent, and duration of the audits in the program.

First-party (internal) audits are planned, conducted, and reported differently than audit types. And internal audit is a separate and independent department. Internal audit often reports up to the Board of Directors audit committee. Internal audit of Quality Management Systems, Environmental Management Systems, as well as others may report up to the Board.

Second-party audits are conducted of suppliers and associated companies. So, client-supplier audits are located in the supply management department or quality department.

Third-party audits are conducted by Certification Bodies for Management System certification. Or, third-party financial audits are conducted of financial firms to provide an opinion on the accuracy of financial reports.

ISO 19011:2018 offers guidance for internal Management System audits, client-supplier audits, and third-party certification audits of Management Systems. ISO 19011:2018 states the guideline can be used of an audit of a single Management System or of a combined Management System.

The size of the audit program may be based on the audit report client requirements and the auditee context. For example, a global organization would have a broad and deep audit program. The audit program of a global organization would audit quality, environment, IT, cyber security, suppliers, operations, quality and every element of the organization including its supply chain. The size of the audit teams can reflect the nature, extent, and complexity of the auditee. For example, a large supplier of complicated technical equipment would have a larger team than an audit of a commodity product supplier.

The extent of the audit program can be based on the types of risks and opportunities that the audit team will encounter during the audit.

Audit programs can become more complicated as more functions and core processes are outsourced. To audit a supplier program, it becomes particularly important to determine where important auditee decisions are made and what constitutes executive management and ownership of the auditee's Management System.

If core auditee functions and processes are outsourced, then the management of the audit program including the design of the planning, conducting, and reporting of the audit becomes more critical. The audit would require more supervision to ensure adequacy and accuracy. Individual audit planning may need to be verified and validated by the audit client and audit management.

In a less complex organization, the audit program would be smaller based on the needs of the audit client. The audit program may be one person in a small company.

An important concept in the latest revisions of ISO standards is the concept of context. There are two types of context: internal and external. External context of an organization encompasses elements such as geography, culture, client requirements, audits, government regulations, and other audit elements. Internal context of the organization includes culture, ethics, tone at the top, and audit internal elements.

In planning the audit program, the audit manager should consider:

- Customer audit requirements.
- Expectations, requirements, and needs of stakeholders and interested parties.
- Audit organization objectives.
- External and internal context including culture, ethic, environment, and business model.
- Confidentiality, security, custody, retention, and ownership requirements.

The audit program manager plans the overall audit program focusing on internal organizational objectives.

The audit program manager is responsible for ensuring that the independence of the audit organization and objectivity of each audit are maintained.

The audit manager risk-manages the audit program. This means that resources, and people are focused on the Management System with the highest inherent risk, lower performance areas, complex products, high risk suppliers, higher expectations, or weak control areas.

Audit team leads should have the appropriate knowledge skills and abilities to lead, plan, conduct, and report audit results.

The audit program manager should identify resources, Information Technology, monies, and people so that audits can be planned, conducted, and reported effectively, efficiently, economically and in a timely manner.

The audit program manager should gather the following information regarding the organization's audits:

a. **Audit program objectives**
   Audit program has auditing objectives, such as who is going to be audited against what Management System requirements.

b. **Risks and opportunities**
   Audit program has associated risks and opportunities. The audit manager can list activities to ensure internal audit organization risks and opportunities can be identified.

c. **Audit scope**
   Audit manager can identify auditees; gather resources; understand the audit boundaries; identify locations; identify audit personnel and leads; and determine critical elements of each audit within the program.

d. **Audit schedule**
   Audit manager can determine a schedule of audits including frequency, duration, purpose, and objectives of each audit.

e. **Audits types**
   Audit manager can Identify each type of audit, including internal, second-party, or third-party audits.

f. **Audit criteria**
   Audit manager can ensure the audit team can identify audit criteria which are the requirements the auditor evaluates to determine adherence against required criteria. Criteria are incorporated into an audit objective.

g. **Audit methods**
   Auditor manager can ensure that appropriate audit methods are identified for each audit. Audit methods are how an audit is planned, conducted, and reported. Audit methods ensure how each audit objective can be fulfilled.

h. **Criteria for choosing team members**
   Audit manager can ensure the audit program has a process for selecting audit team leads and audit members. The criteria should be documented to support evidence-based decisions in the audit.

i. **Documented audit information**
   Audit manager should ensure that above program criteria are developed.

Some of the above information may not be identified until a detailed audit plan for a specific audit is completed.

The audit manager or supervisor has the authority and responsibility to manage and monitor the audit program. ISO 19011:2018 requires the audit program is monitored and measured against its objectives. The audit manager does this routinely. However, a peer review group may be tasked to independently verify and validate that audits are monitored, measured against objectives, and reported on an ongoing basis. Audit program is reviewed to identify changes and possible opportunities for improvement.

ISO 19011:2018 follows a plan, do, check, and act cycle. The critical elements in each phase are identified below:

Plan:

5.2 - Establishing Audit Program Objectives

5.3 - Determining and Evaluating Audit Program Risks and Opportunities

5.4 - Establishing the Audit Program

6.2 - Initiating the Audit

6.3 - Preparing the Audit Activities

Do:

5.5 - Implementing the Audit Program

6.4 - Conducting the Audit Activities

6.5 - Preparing and Distributing the Audit Report

Check:

5.6 - Monitoring the Audit Program

6.6 - Completing the Audit

Act:

5.7 - Reviewing and Improving the Audit Program

6.7 - Conducting the Audit Follow Up

Commentary: This section of the guideline refers to the audit program. First time readers should not get confused with the management of individual audits. While there are similarities, this clause refers to the management of the entire audit program.

5.2 ESTABLISHING AUDIT PROGRAM OBJECTIVES

The audit client has audit program requirements. The audit client is called audit client in ISO 19011:2011. These requirements become the audit objectives.

The client establishes and defines the audit requirements. Interestingly, ISO 19011:2018 states that the audit program can be implemented effectively and under certain conditions the audit client may provide input. The audit client may offer suggestions into audit planning, conducting, and reporting. Audit program objectives can be consistent with the audit client's strategic direction and support Management System policies and procedures.

Audit program objectives can be based on the following:

a. **Needs and Expectations**
   Customer, stakeholder, and interested party requirements, needs, and expectations initiate the audit. Interested parties can be external and internal to the organization.

b. **Characteristics**

Customer audit needs and requirements can be based on project, process, product, and service characteristics. Changes in these can initiate an audit.

c. **Management System requirements**

Management Systems have specific program, process, product, service, and transactional requirements.

d. **External assessment**

External suppliers may initiate development of audit program objectives.

e. **Auditee's performance**

Auditee's Key Performance Indicators (KPI's), Key Risk Indicators (KPI's), Management System maturity, recurrence of findings, and recurrence of corrective actions may initiate audit program objectives.

f. **Risk identification**

Auditee risks and opportunities are key to developing audit program objectives.

g. **Previous audits**

Results of previous audits can impact audit program objectives.

Audit program objectives can be broad and include many audit objective criteria. Audit program objective examples may include:

- Identification of opportunities for improvement of a Management System.
- Identification of opportunities for performance improvement.
- Evaluation of audit program risk controls.

- Evaluation of the auditee's capability to evaluate context appropriately.
- Evaluation of the auditee's capability to determine risks and opportunities and effectively achieve them.
- Evaluation of the auditee's ability to address opportunities and risks, new requirements, conformance of statutory and regulatory requirements; and conformance of the Management System 'shalls.'
- Ability to obtain competence in the supplier to provide conforming products.
- Determination of the suitability, accuracy, effectiveness, efficiency, and economics of the audit Management System.
- Evaluation of the alignment of the Management System objectives against those of the strategic direction of the auditee's organization.

Commentary: Develop yearly objectives and a plan for your first-party, second-party, and third-party auditing. From this plan, you can determine your resource requirements.

5.3 DETERMINING AND EVALUATING AUDIT PROGRAM RISKS AND OPPORTUNITIES

The design of an audit program should be based on the context of the auditee and the organization conducting in the audit. The auditing organization for a large company with thousands of suppliers would be different than for a small business. If the audit team has a complex product or service, the audit will take longer than required. If the audit falls under statutes or regulations, then the audit will be broader, deeper, and take longer than an audit of a commodity supplier.

Risks and opportunities can impact the auditing organization. The audit manager can identify potential audit risks and opportunities when developing the audit plan and share these with the audit client. The audit manager can communicate potential risks and opportunities to the organization's senior management. The audit manager will consider risks and opportunities in terms of the audit program and its resource requirements.

Every audit has risks and opportunities. Risks and opportunities are correlated to the context the auditee. Risks and opportunities impact the achievement of an auditor organization's objectives.

Audit risks should be identified including:

a. **Planning**
   Audits should focus on planning specifically in terms of developing SMART (Specific, Measurable, Attainable, Relevant and Timely) audit objectives. Audit objectives can relate to critical issues of the organization and be mapped to its business plan and business model. Planning can include and consider the following risks: audit objectives, number of audits, duration of audits, and audit location.

b. **Resources**
   Resources including time, people, equipment, training, technical experts, and audit items must be secured for planning, conducting, and reporting the audit.

c. **Selection of the audit team**
   Selection of the audit team is critical for ensuring there are

sufficient members of the team to cover the audit scope completely. The composition and competence of the audit team should reflect the requirements and expectations of the audit.

d. **Audit communication**

Audit communications is critical for understanding audit stakeholder and interested party requirements and to communicate audit results to the stakeholders appropriately in a timely manner.

e. **Implementation**

Audit implementation is called conducting the audit or audit fieldwork. Implementation is critical for ensuring that all moving parts of the audit are effective, efficient, and economic. Information security and confidentiality of information are key in this process.

f. **Control of documented information**

Audit team will review proprietary, sensitive, and confidential information. It is critical this documented information is retained and if necessary encrypted. Critical information may also have to be retained based on statutory or retention requirements.

g. **Monitoring, reviewing, and improvement of the audit program**

The overall audit program is monitored to ensure that audit outcomes meet client requirements. Program monitoring can review the effectiveness, efficiency, and economics of the audit program and individual audits. Monitoring, reviewing, and improving form lessons learned feedback loop.

h. **Availability**

Audits can only be conducted if the auditee is cooperating with the audit team, for example providing evidence to the audit team; providing access to electronic communications; providing desk space; ensuring the right people are available to be interviewed; and providing record samples and evidence as requested.

Commentary: ISO 19011: 2018 is a major update from the previous standard. The organization updating its audit program based on this new standard will find there are many opportunities for improvement and for updating its current audit program.

Opportunities may for improvement of the audit program may include:

- Developing audits teams that will be able to conduct multiple Management System audits and a single audit.
- Minimizing time and effort traveling to the auditee site.
- Balancing knowledge, skills, and abilities of the audit team to the requisites of specific audit objectives.
- Ensuring that audit balances the availability of the audit team and the auditee's key personnel needed to be available and interviewed.
- Identify audit areas or suppliers that pose the highest risk.

5.4 ESTABLISHING AUDIT PROGRAM

5.4 1 ROLES AND RESPONSIBILITIES OF INDIVIDUAL(S) MANAGING THE AUDIT PROGRAM

Multiple people or a single person may manage the audit program. These individuals have roles, responsibilities, and authorities which are key requirements for successful audits. These manager (s) are responsible for:

a. **Audit program scope**
   Establish the scope of the audit program based on audit objectives and any known hindrances or risks to the audit program.

b. **External and internal issues**
   Review the internal and external audit context, constraints, risks, and opportunities that can impact the audit program. Once identified, audit management can implement actions to; eliminate constraints, mitigate risks, and take advantage of opportunities.

c. **Selection of audit teams**
   Select appropriate members to the audit team so that audits can be conducted effectively, efficiently, and economically. Audit team selection involves selecting members, assigning roles, delegating responsibilities, and defining key tasks.

d. **Relevant processes**
   Define audit processes for:

   - Coordinating and scheduling all audits within the audit program.

- Identifying audit objectives, scope, and requirements for audit planning, conducting, and reporting.
- Selecting appropriate and competent auditors.
- Developing internal and external communication protocols so audit requirements can be understood as well as results communicated to the appropriate audit stakeholders.
- Developing a resolution process for disagreements among audit team members and auditee. There can be a process for reconciling and reporting disagreements of findings.
- Reporting audit findings to the audit client and interested parties.

e. Determine and provision resources

Identify the resources for ensuring audits can be completed on time, on budget, within scope, and achieving audit objectives.

f. Documented information

Assure that appropriate audit program evidence, data, information can be developed for the audit trail.

g. Monitor and improve audit program

Review audit program performance. If audit performance needs to be improved, then appropriate corrective action is implemented.

h. Communicate audit program

Update executive audit stakeholders on the status of the audit program. As well, communicate audit results to the appropriate stakeholders and interested parties.

Commentary: The above checklist, items a. through h. can become the basis for a yearly audit plan.

5.4.2 COMPETENCE OF INDIVIDUALS MANAGING

The audit program manager should have the necessary knowledge, skills, and abilities to lead the program. The audit program manager can have the ability to understand contextual issues and manage audit risks and opportunities appropriately. The program manager should have the following knowledge, skills, and abilities:

a. **Audit principles, processes, and tools**
   Audit principles provide the generic guidelines for planning, conducting, and reporting an audit; identifying audit processes; and describing the steps of an audit. Methods such as sampling describe the specific steps that are needed to verify and validate audit principles.

b. **Management System standards documents**
   ISO is updating many of its Management System standards, such as ISO 9001:2015 and ISO 14001:2015. ISO 9001:2015 is the Quality Management System standard. ISO 14001:2015 is the Environmental Management System standard. ISO 19011:2018 is the auditing and assurance standard that can be used with all ISO Management System standards.

c. **Auditee contact information**
   The audit team will be visiting the auditee to conduct the audit. The audit team has specific objectives to evaluate. The team needs intimate and specific knowledge of the auditee. Auditee context can change the audit purpose and scope. Context may involve external and internal cultural issues, needs, and

ojects, processes, services, prod-

latory requirements

ations, statutes, and rules that be- quirements of the audit. Auditors iirements.

n members can have knowledge, agement, process management, nology, and cybersecurity.

understand while reading this document that the Management System landscape is changing. Auditors need more knowledge, skills, and abilities to plan, conduct, and report on new Management System standards.

5.4.3 ESTABLISHING THE EXTENT OF THE AUDIT PROGRAM

The program manager needs to define the boundaries of the audit program. Companies are requiring more assurance of their activities, so the audit program is quickly expanding its scope to include supply chain risk management, compliance, cybersecurity, operations, Information Technology, and many audit areas.

In a small company, the audit program may consist of only one person with additional responsibilities. Care should be taken that the audit manager has responsibilities and audit responsibilities that do not conflict or create an appearance of a conflict of interest.

The boundaries of the audit program can include the following factors:

a. **Audit objective**

Purpose, scope, duration of each audit; number of audits conducted; types of reports, time of the audit, and cost of the audits can influence audit program objectives.

b. **Management System standards**

Management System standards, requirements, and audit criteria can impact the boundaries of the audit program.

c. **Number of audits**

Number of audits; criticality of the audit; locations of the audits; complexity of the processes and or products being assessed; processes being audited can add resources, time, people requirements can modify audit program boundaries.

d. **Management System standards**

Consideration of the inhibitors, effectiveness, efficiency, and economics of the Management System can modify the audit program boundaries.

e. **Audit criteria**

Appropriate and specific audit criteria and requirements are defined for each type of Management System audit. Different types of audits may be conducted such as Management System, statutory, product, service, project, and process audits. Each of these audits has different audit criteria, requirements, and objectives.

f. **Previous audit results**

Outcomes of previous audits, including first-party, second-party, and third-party audits will impact current audits. If previous audits had critical findings, then the boundaries of the audit program may expand to reflect these risks.

g. Previous audit program results

Results of peer reviews and audit evaluations of the entire audit program can change the boundaries of the audit program.

h. Language and culture

Ethical, cultural, political, social, and audit contextual factors. Contextual factors may be internal and external to the organization.

i. Interested party concerns

Audit stakeholders, clients, and interested parties may have special needs and requirements of the audit program. These special requirements should be understood, written down, and discussed with all interested parties.

j. Changes in context

Significant changes in audit context may change audit boundaries. Significant changes may include changes in auditee operations, new management, new risks, new opportunities, new business model and audit changes that may impact audit scope.

k. Information availability

New ways of planning, conducting, and reporting the audit can also change audit boundaries. Depending on audit requirements, audits may be conducted remotely or through the use of new Information Technologies.

l. Event recurrence

Internal and or external events can change program audit boundaries. Black swans are events that have high impact and consequence but a relatively low likelihood of occurring. These events can change the scope of an audit program. It is important for the audit team to be prepared for these types of events.

m. **Business risks and opportunities**
Business risks and opportunities and how to remediate them. The audit program can proactively pursue opportunities. The audit program can also proactively and preventively mitigate risks.

Commentary: Do not try to boil the ocean or in other words scope your audit to what is required in the Management System. The new Management Systems are broadly written and more interpretive. We strongly recommend that you tighten the scope of the audit to required audit objectives.

5.4.4 DETERMINING AUDIT PROGRAM RESOURCES

Audit programs require significant resources including monies, people, Information Technology, process (audit) rules, support personnel, technical specialists, senior management support, and other resources. The audit manager should consider the following when determining audit resources:

a. **Resources**
Resources need to be scheduled to plan, conduct, and report audits results.

b. **Audit methods**
Audits may require a technical specialist to plan, conduct, and report the audit. The specialist may use special methods to analyze data or conduct special test.

c. **Auditor availability**

Auditors and a technical specialist should be available to conduct the audit and meet its particular objectives.

d. **Audit program scope**

Risks and opportunities can impact the extent and scope of the audit program. High risks and opportunities would expand the audit program.

e. **Travel expenses**

Audit scheduling and travel costs may impact the audit. Offshore audits are more expensive than down the street.

f. **Time zone impacts**

Impact of different time zones especially if it is a second-party, offshore audit may require additional resources.

g. **Information availability**

Availability of data required to conduct audits would expand or confine the scope of the audit.

h. **Tool availability**

Availability of Information Technology or audit equipment to conduct the audit can impact scope. For example, a product review may require specific tools. A process audit may require flow charts. Cyber security audit may require access to access control plans.

i. **Documented information availability**

Availability of information may require massive amounts of information to be evaluated. For example, an evaluation of purchasing may require access to thousands of purchasing invoices to be examined that will be specifically sampled to determine compliance with procedures.

j. **Facility requirements**
   Customer, facility, government/regulatory, or sensitive audit requirements may require security clearances, equipment, non-disclosure agreements, background checks, protective clothing, etc.

Commentary: At the start of your budgeting cycle, plan your audits and request resources to complete the plan. You will find that the new Management Systems require additional efforts, time, and monies.

5.5 IMPLEMENTING AUDIT PROGRAM

5.5.1 GENERAL

Once the audit program has been established, it must be implemented. Implementation often means developing and overall strategy, tactics, and plans for implementing the audit program.

The audit manager should consider the following when implementing the audit program:

a. **Communication**
   Communicate possible risks and opportunities for improvement in the audit program to relevant stakeholders, clients, and interested parties. As well, the audit manager should monitor the progress of the audit program and report these to audit stakeholders.

b. **Objectives**
   Define the scope, requirements, criteria, and objectives of each individual audit to audit stakeholders.

c. **Audit methods**

Define audit methods in each audit plan. Audit methods to achieve audit objectives are defined in the planning phase.

d. **Schedule audit**

Coordinate and schedule audits and audit activities of the audit. The audit team lead schedules the audit sufficiently early so the audit team and auditee are prepared for the audit.

e. **Auditor competence**

Ensure the entire audit team has the necessary knowledge, skills, and abilities to plan, conduct, and report the specific audit. If not, the audit team lead is also responsible for securing technical specialists.

f. **Resources**

Ensure that each audit team has necessary resources including monies, people, equipment, etc. If not, the audit team lead is responsible for securing the requisite resources.

g. **Audit program**

Ensure individual audits are planned, conducted, and reported in accordance with audit program policies and procedures. Audit risks, opportunities, and issues are identified prior to the audit. If there are unexpected risks, sufficient resources are available to resolve them or at least to mitigate their impacts.

h. **Documented information**

Ensure that audit program policies and procedures are current and maintained. Audit program maintains a master manual of policies and procedures. They are maintained and updated as required.

i. **Operational controls**
   Ensure adequate audit program controls are designed and implemented to ensure audit program monitoring and assurance.

j. **Audit program review**
   Review the audit program periodically to identify opportunities for improvement and manage risks preemptively.

Commentary: ISO 19011:2018 and the new Management Systems incorporate context, risk, and other requirements. More than ever: Plan your audits - Audit to your plan.

5.5.2 DEFINING THE OBJECTIVES, SCOPE, AND CRITERIA FOR AN INDIVIDUAL AUDIT

Each individual audit has different objectives, requirements, and scope. The audit team lead is responsible for defining the objectives, scope, and audit criteria of each audit. Each audit is treated as a separate audit. Each audit can be planned, conducted, and reported following a similar process. Outcomes and results will be different for each audit.

The audit objective defines what the audit will be evaluating. An objective may consist of the following:

a. **Extent of conformity**
   Determining extent of conformity of a Management System being audited. This includes audit criteria and requirements.

b. **Management System capability**
   Determination of the Management System effectiveness to meet statutory and regulatory requirements or audit organizational requirements.

c. **Management System effectiveness**
Determination of the effectiveness, efficiency, and economics of the Management System in meeting its intended purposes.

d. **Opportunities for Improvement**
Identification of opportunities for improvement in the Management System or processes.

e. **Suitability and completeness**
Evaluation of the appropriateness of the Management System based on an evaluation of organizational context, strategic direction, business model, and core processes of the auditee.

Audit lead should evaluate the capability of the Management System to achieve its objectives. Critical part of this definition is to address risks and opportunities within the organization. As well if there is a changing context, then the capability and maturity the Management System should be reevaluated.

Audit scope is determined by cost, schedule, quality, and technology factors.

Audit criteria which were defined earlier is the point at which adherence to conformance is evaluated. Audit criteria may include the following: policies, procedures, work instructions, Key Performance Indicators, Key Risk Indicators, processing, statutory requirements, financial requirements, cyber security requirements, risks, and opportunities for enhancement.

Changes to audit objectives, scope, criteria, references, or requirements, may require a change management process. The audit program or the individual audit scope may have to be changed. If there are audit changes, these are communicated to interested parties such as audit client, audit, and interested parties.

Sometimes more than one Management System, function, or discipline is audited. The audit team must be aware of the audit objectives, scope, criteria of each Management System, function, and discipline. This is critical because one part of the audit may focus on the enterprise, while parts of the audit may focus at the programmatic, project, or process level. Or, an audit may simply evaluate transactions and products or services the auditee provides.

Commentary: Make the audit process as straight forward as possible with templates, checklists, and other auditing tools. They will really help you with the audits.

5.5.3 SELECTING AND DETERMINING METHODS

The audit manager or the audit team lead selects and determines the appropriate methods for effectively, efficiently, and economically conducting the audit. This determination is based on audit requirements, objectives, scope, and criteria.

Audits can be planned, conducted, and reported at the client's site, auditee's site, or remotely. Remotely implies that communications among the audit team are via email or electronically. The determination of the appropriate method is based on associated risks and opportunities for each audit.

Occasionally, two or more auditing groups will conduct a joint audit of the same auditee. Two different clients may audit suppliers simultaneously. Each client will have a separate audit team, requirements, criteria, and scope. It is critical that the joint teams agree on audit methods and protocols prior to the audit and communicate these to the auditee. Also, if two or more Management Systems such as Information Security and Quality Management are being audited, then two different teams from one client may be involved in the joint audit.

Commentary: Use the appropriate audit method to get the requisite information for each audit objective. This implies that the auditor may use different methods for each objective.

5.5.4 SELECTING AUDIT TEAM MEMBERS

The audit manager appoints team audit team leads. The audit team leads select individual team members. As well, audit team leads may select technical experts to support specific audits.

The audit team lead selects members based on audit objectives, audit context, individual member knowledge, skills, and abilities, and a number of audit factors. It can be mentioned that many Management System audits are conducted by only one auditor. This person becomes the audit team lead.

During the audit planning phase, the knowledge, skills, and abilities needed among the team members to achieve audit objectives should be identified. It is important to select audit team members based on the requisite abilities of the team to plan, conduct, and report the audit.

A critical issue is the size and composition of the overall audit team. For complex audits, the team can be large and diverse with specific skills. For a narrow audit scope, the audit team may be small or even one person.

Factors to consider in selecting audit team members include:

a. **Audit team competence**
Most critical factor to consider in selecting audit team members includes the overall knowledge, skills, and abilities of the audit team to achieve the audit objectives based on specific criteria. Other audit considerations also include: audit scope, technology, process capability, and other audit factors.

b. **Audit complexity**
Technical, complexity, and domain knowledge of the auditee impact audit team selection. Complexity may involve technology, process, product, project, and process factors.

c. **Audit type**
Audit team selection also depends on whether it is a single or combined audit evaluating multiple Management Systems.

d. **Audit method**
Determination of appropriate audit methods is based on audit objectives. Depending on the audit objective, different methods may be used to conduct the audit. The audits method can be selected in the planning phase of the audit.

e. **Conflict of interest**
Audit team should avoid direct or any appearance of conflicts of interest in planning, conducting, and reporting the audit. The team should review possible stakeholders of the audit report and determine if they have any specific conflict-of-interest requirements, such as non-disclosure agreement to be signed by team members.

f. **Work effectively**
Audit team should work together closely in planning, conducting, and reporting the audit. The audit team lead should be able to work well with the auditee and interested parties.

g. **Audit context**
Some auditee's has special contextual requirements that may limit audit team effectiveness. Audits may have special contextual requirements such as language, Information Technology, special processes, or specific knowledge domain requirements. Context refers to the external and internal environment, culture, and ethics surrounding the audit. Politics and culture may also be important contextual characteristics. Contextual audit issues should be addressed prior to conducting the audit preferably in the planning phase.

a. **Audit complexity**
Technology and security issues must be addressed prior to being on-site and conducting the audit.

Contextual issues both external and internal of the auditee should be identified and addressed prior to the audit. These issues may involve language culture, ethics, and audit critical factors.

The audit manager or team lead decides who can be on the team. Audit team members should reflect the needs of the audit, its objectives, and the special context of the auditee. The audit manager can consult with an audit team lead on the composition and selection of the audit team for each specific audit.

Audits may require technical experts or specialists. These experts can be available to support the audit team lead. As well, the audit team lead can explain requirements and expectations to the technical experts.

In many companies, Management System auditing is an area where operational experts may be assigned as observers or auditors in training. The audit team lead is responsible for providing appropriate guidance for these professionals.

The audit team lead should ask each team member and technical expert assigned to the team if there is any appearance or potential conflict of interest. Conflict of interest and similar Issues can be identified and resolved prior to conducting the audit on-site.

Commentary: If you work for a small company, the person assigned to Management System audit is also the audit manager and audit lead.

5.5.5 ASSIGNING RESPONSIBILITY TO THE AUDIT TEAM LEADER

The audit manager should formally assign responsibility, accountabilities, and authorities for conducting an individual audit to the audit team lead. Assigning responsibility should be made sufficiently early so the team lead can prepare for the audit.

The audit manager can share the following information with the audit team lead:

a. **Audit objectives**
   Audit client requirements and audit objectives can be defined early so the audit team lead has sufficient time to prepare and obtain resources.

b. **Audit criteria**

Audit criteria, requirements, standards, and any relevant information are also identified sufficiently early. To evaluate audit criteria, specialists, equipment, or gages may be required.

c. **Audit scope**

Audit scope including organizational functions, projects, processes, programs, services, activities, and products can be established and evaluated in the planning phase.

d. **Audit processes**

Audit processes for conducting the audit are mapped to specific audit requirements and objectives.

e. **Audit team composition**

Composition of the audit team may include audit team lead, members, technical experts, and observers. The team reflects the needs and requirements of the audit.

f. **Contract details**

Auditee information, location, time frame, duration and details required to conduct the audit are gathered early.

g. **Audit resources**

Additional requirements or personal necessary to plan, conduct, and report the audit are identified.

h. **Risks and opportunities**

Expectations and requirements can be identified for addressing risks and opportunities throughout the audit including planning, conducting, and reporting the audit.

i. **Audit team lead support**

Relevant knowledge and data that would support the audit

team in achieving its objectives and working with the auditee are also identified.

Each audit follows a similar process, specifically planning, conducting, and reporting the audit. However, each audit is different in terms of the auditee processes, audit requirements, objectives, audit criteria, and methods for conducting the audit.

Audit manager should determine audit assignments, responsibilities, and accountabilities before the audit and may cover the following:

- Audit, such as a client-supplier audit, may involve offshore evaluations and auditee visits. Several challenges may arise. There may be differences in language between the auditor and auditee. In such cases, an interpreter or local facility facilitator may be necessary.
- Audit report distribution should be considered early on and be part of the scope of the audit.
- Proprietary, confidential, private, and classified information may be encountered during the audit. These matters can be discussed and resolved with the auditee and client prior to the audit.
- Sustainability, environmental, safety, and health requirements and responses from the audit team should be discussed with the auditee. For example, is there a possibility the audit team may be exposed to hazardous substances.
- Access to secure sites should be discussed with the auditee and preparations should be made sufficiently early for site visits during the planning phase of the audit.

- Authorization and approval of security requirements should be addressed during the planning phase.
- Subsequent review following audit findings may be required. Corrective action may require a subsequent review. These should be discussed with the auditee and audit client.
- Audit may consist of activities that are being conducted simultaneously such as planning, conducting, and reporting the audit. The audit team lead should coordinate these activities with the team and the auditee.
- Audit team leads in a joint audit should work together and coordinate activities throughout the audit. This is crucial to ensure that the auditee does not have to respond to the same questions from two different team leads which will result in confusion. The audit team lead should specify specific activities for each team member as well as time frames with each audit team member.

Commentary: Audit team leads are the key element for a successful Management System audit. Ensure they know how to plan, conduct, and report a Risk Based Audit.

5.5.6 MANAGING AUDIT PROGRAM RESULTS

The audit manager is responsible for ensuring that the following activities are performed effectively, efficiently, and economically:

a. **Audit objectives**
   Evaluate audit objectives are achieved for each audit within the audit program.

b. **Audit report approval**
   Review of each audit finding and approve the final audit report.

c. **Audit finding review**
   Review the applicability, scope, and suitability of the audit findings.

d. **Audi report distribution**
   Determine appropriate distribution of audit reports to the client, appropriate stakeholders, and interested parties.

e. **Follow up audit**
   Determine if a follow-up audit is required for approving or reviewing corrective actions or opportunities for improvement.

Audit manager can apply audit results to areas of the organization so that audit recommendations can be replicated and scaled within the organization.

Audit manager should communicate specific audit results, observations, best practices, and opportunities for improvement to areas in the organization in a first-party audit.

5.5.7 MANAGING AND MAINTAINING AUDIT PROGRAM RECORDS

Audit manager is responsible for ensuring that each audit is supported sufficiently so that an independent third-party would reach the same conclusions as the audit the audit team or individual auditor. This requires that decision or audit trail is developed.

Each audit has audit records and evidence for supporting each finding that is mapped to each audit objective. Audit evidence can be generated, managed, maintained, managed, and stored for a specific determination. Many companies have retention policies for audit records. Especially with proprietary, confidential, and classified information, the organization should have a specific audit retention policy.

Information and records may include:

a. **Audit program information**
   Audit program information such as:

   - List of audits. List of areas to be audited.
   - Audit schedule. Overall audit program objectives linked to strategic objectives.
   - Audit program context, risks, and opportunities.
   - Third-party review of audit program effectiveness, efficiency, and economics.

b. **Records**
   Information and records regarding each audit, such as:

   - Individual audit scope plans, details on audit conduct, and similar reports.
   - Objectives of each audit.
   - Evidence gathered in each audit.
   - Findings of each audit mapped to audit objectives.
   - List of findings and non-conformity reports.
   - Corrective action reports and or preventive action reports.

- Opportunities for improvement if appropriate.
- Recommendations for follow-up review, reports, or audit.

c. **Audit team information**

Information regarding the audit team, such as: knowledge, skills, and abilities of the audit team lead and members. Appraisal of each audit and overall direction of the audit program may involve:

- Reviewing audit team effectiveness and audit team lead effectiveness.
- Updating and improving overall audit program competence and capability of audit team members.
- Reviewing individual audit records so they are sufficient and suitable to allow a third-party to evaluate the overall program and to evaluate the effectiveness of each audit finding.

5.6 MONITORING AUDIT PROGRAM

Audit manager should periodically evaluate the effectiveness, efficiency, and economics of the audit program. In some cases, a third-party may be asked to conduct a peer review of the audit program. The following should be evaluated regarding the audit program:

a. **Audit schedules**

Audit program schedule, costs, quality, scope and responsibilities are being met. Individual audit schedule, cost, quality, scope and audit objectives are being met.

b. **Audit team performance**
   Audit team lead and members and technical experts are evaluated periodically.

c. **Audit team plan**
   Audit plan is sufficiently clear so the team can conduct the audit according to plan.

d. **Audit feedback**
   Audit team lead surveys audit clients, audits, and audit interested parties to ensure that expectations, and needs are being met.

e. **Audit documentation suitability**
   Reliable documented information is available for the entire audit program and processes.

The audit program should be flexible. Factors may impinge that require the audit program to be modified. Several changes that may impact and audit program include:

- New types of audits requiring a revision of some or all the audit methods.
- Audit findings of complex auditee systems or processes.
- Different types of Management System with a different level of maturity. Effectiveness, efficiency, and economics of the audit program.
- Expansion or contraction of the audit program or individual audit scope.
- Changes or disruption to the audit Management System.

- Changes to the standards, context, requirements, or criteria to which the audit is evaluating.
- Changes of suppliers or external providers of services or products.
- Potential conflicts of interest.
- Scope changes by the audit client or stakeholder.

Commentary: Conduct every three years a peer review of the Management System audit program.

5.7 REVIEWING AND IMPROVING THE AUDIT PROGRAM

The audit manager should periodically review the audit program for possible improvement. First, the program has specific Key Performance Indicators. The audit manager should review the objectives to ensure that they are being met. As well, some organizations may rely on a third-party to conduct an independent assessment of the audit program. Whether it is the audit manager or an independent third-party auditor can develop lessons learned or develop opportunities for improvement regarding the audit program.

The audit program manager is responsible for the following:

- Review of the overall goals of the audit program and make sure that they are aligned with organizational strategy and plans.
- Identify areas and opportunities for improvement and value creation.

- Modify the audit program based on input from the lessons learned evaluation or from the opportunities from improvement that have been identified.

- Continually review knowledge, skills, and abilities of the audit team leads and auditors.

The audit program manager is responsible for reporting the results of the audit program review to upper management. If there are opportunities for improvement, then they can be applied with a subsequent analysis to determine and type and levels of improvement.

The audit program review may consider the following:

a. **Results and trends**
   Quality, cost, and audit trends of the audit program throughout the years.

b. **Audit process conformity**
   Benchmark the audit program against audits in similar Industries.

c. **Needs and expectation**
   Determine if audit program processes and technology conform with company requirements and can be improved through best practices.

d. **Audit program records**
   Determine the requirements, needs, and expectations, of audit clients, stakeholders, and interested parties.

e. **New audit methods**
   Determine if audit program records are suitable, sufficient, accurate, and reliable.

f. **New audit review method**

Review if new auditing methods may be applied within the organization.

g. **Risks and opportunities**

Review effectiveness, efficiency, and economics regarding risks and opportunities for improving the overall audit program.

h. **Confidentiality**

Determine compliance with company requirements for securing confidential, proprietary, classified, and sensitive information regarding internal, client, and auditee information.

Commentary: ISO 19011:2018 is a major departure from the previous standard. Ensure your audit leads and auditors are trained to the new standard.

6. CONDUCTING THE AUDIT

6.1 GENERAL

There are three critical elements in a Management System audit: 1. Planning; 2. Conducting; and 3. Reporting. ISO 19011:2018 covers these three elements of the audit. It should be mentioned that ISO 19011:2018 refers to planning as initiating the audit. The information in this clause can be applied to the general design of an audit program. As well, the guideline states that the sequence, specific activities, and length of time for these activities needs to be tailored to the context of the auditee and the requirements and objectives of the audit.

6.2 INITIATING THE AUDIT

6.2.1 GENERAL

The audit team lead is responsible and has the authority for conducting the audit.

6.2.2 ESTABLISHING CONTACT WITH THE AUDITEE

The audit team lead is responsible for contacting the auditee. The following may be discussed in the initial conversation:

a. **Communication protocols**
   Discuss with a client and the auditee the required communication protocols.

b. **Audit authority**
Confirm with the client and the auditee the basis for the authority and purpose for conducting the audit.

c. **Audit team members**
Determine audit objectives, requirements, criteria, methods, and scope with the auditee. The composition of the audit team including any type of coal expert should be discussed as well.

d. **Access permission**
Obtain permission from the auditee to access facilities for planning, conducting, and reporting the audit.

e. **Statutory requirements**
Review any applicable statutory requirements to the audit. Discuss with the auditee how to determine how to demonstrate compliance with these regulatory requirements.

f. **Confidential information handling**
Negotiate with the auditee transparency, disclosure, and dissemination of proprietary, confidential, or secret information.

g. **Audit scheduling**
Determine the timing and scope of the audit with auditee. Ensure that the right people are available for conducting the audit.

h. **Safety and health issues**
Review access or security constraints to conducting the audit.

i. **Observers**
Negotiate the attendance of technical experts or audit professionals on the audit team and ensure access to secure locations.

j. **Auditee risk areas**
   Discuss with the auditee any risks or opportunities that may result from the audit.

k. **Issue resolution**
   Negotiate and resolve conflicting issues with the auditee and the client prior to conducting the audit.

6.2.3 DETERMINING FEASIBILITY OF THE AUDIT

The audit team lead along with team members should determine if the audit can be planned, conducted, and reported suitably. Every audit involves constraints and each element or phase of the audit. The audit manager and audit team lead must have sufficient competence that the audit can be conducted within budget, schedule, quality, and cost.

Factors to consider in determining the feasibility the audit may include:

a. **Audit information availability**
   Availability of information, data, and audit information appropriate resources for planning, conducting, and reporting the audit.

b. **Auditee cooperation**
   Suitable coordination and cooperation from the auditee.

c. **Audit time adequacy**
   Sufficient time, information, technology, processes, people, and resources for planning, conducting, and reporting the audit.

If the above are not available, an agreement should be developed with a client and the auditee regarding suitability and sufficiency of resources.

6.3 PREPARING AUDIT ACTIVITIES

6.3.1 PERFORMING REVIEW OF DOCUMENTED INFORMATION

Each Management System should have evidence that it is complying with the requirements of the Management System. Traditionally, Management System documentation may involve policies, procedures, and work instructions. For example, Quality Management System would have a quality manual or similar documentation with all this information. Or, Quality Management System documented information may involve data or process flowcharts. The auditor still needs documentation to be reviewed to determine compliance or satisfaction to the requirements or audit criteria.

The auditor is responsible for conducting a review of the following documented information:

a. **Gather auditee information**
   Secure sufficient information to understand the auditee's business model, plans, functions, projects, and processes in order to conduct the audit adequately. As well, the auditor needs to secure documented information to support his or her reasoning regarding a finding. Sometimes, this is called an audit trail.

b. **Identify areas of concern**
   Gather adequate and sufficient information to determine conformance against audit criteria or determine whether an audit

objective has been met. If there are possible areas of confusion or a concern, they should be brought up with the auditee. If they cannot be ascertained or resolved with the auditee, then there should be an escalation mechanism for resolving possible misunderstandings or deficiencies.

The auditor requires documented information as evidence to support his or her findings. The evidence can be original documentation or records. Or, evidence may be documentation secured from previous audits.

A new concept that is found in ISO 19011:2018 is context. The size, type, extent, and completeness of required information can be based on auditee's context. For example, a review of a statutory product would entail more documented information then a review of a simple product attributes.

A concept that is also woven throughout the document is risks and opportunities which can dictate audit scope, objectives, criteria, and requirements.

6.3 PREPARING AUDIT ACTIVITIES

6.3.1 PERFORMING REVIEW OF DOCUMENTED INFORMATION

Each Management System should have documented information that is generated by the auditee. The auditor uses the auditee's documentation and information as evidence to support a finding or conclusion based on an audit objective.

The auditor preparing to visit the auditee's site can:

- Gather sufficient and suitable information regarding the auditee's business model, processes, operations, projects, and products/services to understand the auditee's context.
- Develop an overview and checklist of the Management System documentation to scope out the extent and depth of audit opportunities and risks for conducting the audit.
- Secure Management System records which may include previous audit reports, internal audit reports, auditee policies, procedures, work instructions, design drawings, process diagrams, decision flow charts, and audit requisite information. The type, nature, and extent of information security depends on the context of the auditee.

6.3.2 AUDIT PLANNING

6.3.2.1 RISK-BASED APPROACH TO PLANNING

The auditor Is now required to follow a risk-based approach to planning the audit. Risk-based approach is new to ISO 19011:2018. The risk based approach is based on the context of the audit client and the context of the auditee.

A risk-based approach to audit planning involves identifying the critical activities in the audit that may impact the audit's planning, conducting, and reporting. Audit client, audit team, and auditee can develop an understanding regarding these risks and how they may be mitigated during the conduct of the audit.

Much planning can be a straightforward process of scheduling, costing, scoping, and coordinating the activities in an efficient, effective, and economic matter.

The risk-based audit plan should be based on the auditee's context. If an auditee's organization has global, complex, and extensive processes, then the audit plan should reflect this. If the auditee's organization is fairly simple then the audit plan will reflect this and would be a shorter document.

The amount of detail in the audit plan should be based on the context of the auditee. In developing the audit plan, the audit team lead may consider the following:

a. **Audit team composition**
   Composition of the audit team and its overall knowledge, skills, and capabilities to complete the audit. Broader and more complex audit requires a broader team.

b. **Sampling techniques**
   Amount of evidence to gather through sampling. Part of evidence-gathering is determining if sampling is required. Sampling is conducted if the audit requires a higher level of assurance.

c. **Effectiveness and improvement**
   Opportunities to improve the effectiveness, efficiency, and economics of conducting the audit enhance audit risk assurance.

d. **Audit objective risks**
   Risk of not achieving audit objectives due to ineffective audit planning, conducting and reporting.

e. **Auditee risks**
   Auditor while planning, conducting, and reporting the audit may pose risks to the auditee's operations.

Commentary: ISO 19011:2018 integrates risk into planning, conducting, and reporting the audit. Each of the above bullets from a through e should be integrated into the risk plan.

Risks to the auditee can be the result of team members interfering with auditee's operations; adding more risk to health, safety and environment; or impacting adversely the manufacturing of products or the delivering of services. For example, auditors may contaminate a clean room.

In a combined or joint audit, audit team leads should be particularly aware of competing objectives, common processes to be reviewed, access to personnel and areas, and different types of auditing protocols.

6.3.2 AUDIT PLANNING DETAILS

Audit planning is tailored to the requirements of the client, audit processes, audits context, and abilities of the audit team.

Audit planning can be scaled, expanded or contracted based on the following criteria:

a. **Audit objectives**
   More audit objectives require a broader audit scope.

b. **Audit scope**
   Audit scope and constraints. Audit scope is based on the auditee's functions, processes, locations, products, and complexity.

c. **Audit criteria**

Audit criteria and requirements should be linked to strategic objectives.

d. **Audit locations**

Location schedule, scope, duration, cost, personal, Information Technology, and audit factors change the resourcing, time, cost, and assurance requirements of the audit.

e. **Audit team familiarization**

Time necessary for the audit team to become knowledgeable of the auditee's facilities, processes, products, Information Technology, and audit factors may change depending on the scope and context of the audit.

f. **Audit methods used**

Methods for conducting the audit are based on the audit objectives and level of assurance necessary. Higher level of assurance may require sampling strategies in order to obtain sufficient evidence to reach of finding.

g. **Audit team roles and responsibilities**

Audit team authorities, accountabilities, and roles may require the audit team, technical experts, observers, and audit key members.

h. **Resource allocation**

Resources should be linked to audit objectives and available to the audit team so that risks can be minimized and opportunities be enhanced during the audit.

Planning also involves the following:

- Identification of the auditee's support team. The support team provides the audit team with location services, access support, badging, Information Technology access, interviewee assistance, resources, and general audit support.
- If the language between the audit team and the auditee is different, then an interpreter may be required.
- Critical factors in the audit report to be considered beyond those of audit objectives should be identified and resources.
- Accommodations, logistics, communication, technology, and audit assistance may be required for planning, conducting, and reporting the audit.
- Risks to the audit should be identified in the planning phase. Risks can then be minimized. Opportunities can also be enhanced in the planning phase.
- Audit team may require access to secure proprietary, confidential, classified, and sensitive information. This information needs to be secured and retained carefully during the audit based on auditee or statutory requirements.

Audit may require follow-up action based on findings, corrective actions, or opportunities for improvement. Follow up activities are often only known during the conducting and reporting phases of the audit. So, there should be additional planning at each of these stages.

A joint audit may be conducted with the auditee. In such cases the audit team leads there should be coordinated among the audit teams with the auditee.

The audit team lead may share the audit plan with the auditee. If there are conflicts or misunderstandings about the plan, then they should be discussed and resolved before the audit is conducted and reported.

Commentary: Each of the above list of items should be addressed in the audit plan.

6.3.3 ASSIGNING WORK TO THE AUDIT TEAM

Audit team lead is responsible for the overall audit plan and for assigning tasks to each audit team member. Depending on audit team members knowledge, skills, and abilities, the auditor may prepare his or her own audit plan directly related to his or her responsibilities.

Audit team lead determines who, where, and when specific auditee processes, projects, activities, functions, locations, products, and services will be audited. The audit team lead is particularly responsible for ensuring the independence, competence, and objectivity of the auditor assigned to the auditee's location and facility.

During the conduct of the audit, audit team lead will gather members to see if schedule, scope, quality, and cost of the audit are being managed reasonably. If there are changes to the scope of the audit, the lead will ensure there is a change management process and change work assignments accordingly.

6.3.4 PREPARING DOCUMENTED INFORMATION FOR THE AUDIT

Individual audit team members are assigned a particular audit task. Each member identifies critical information to collect and review prior to the audit. The information can relate to each specific audit objective a team member has been assigned.

Documented information is the evidence that the auditor will be collecting during or prior the audit which may include:

a. **Checklists**
   Checklists are the most common tools for conducting the audit. Checklists can be physical or digital.

b. **Sampling plans**
   Populations of data including sampling details.

c. **Audio visual information**
   Critical audit information may be found in audio visual presentations, web, or social media site.

Auditor will report progress and prepare documentation of the audit during the opening auditee meeting, during the audit, and at the closing meetings.

The purpose of collecting this information is to better understand the auditee as well as recognize potential risks in conducting and reporting the audit before they emerge.

The auditor while planning, conducting, and reporting can collect generic and protected information. The retention of this audit information should be filed appropriately and protected. As well, proprietary, confidential, classified, and sensitive information may have to be safeguarded using special measures.

Commentary: Collect as much critical auditee information prior to being onsite for a second-party or third-party audit. This will save you a lot of time and effort.

6.4 CONDUCTING AUDIT ACTIVITIES

6.4.1 GENERAL

The audit is often conducted in a series parallel method. When a single auditor is conducting the audit, then the audit is conducted sequentially. If an audit team is involved in the audit, then different team members will take parallel paths. Each auditor will be involved in different auditee areas conducting different tests and securing information based on different audit criteria. These audits are called series parallel audits.

6.4.2 ASSIGNING ROLES AND RESPONSIBILITIES OF GUIDES AND OBSERVERS

Audit team may have observers, technical experts, interpreters and even guides. These additional members of the audit team may come from the client, regulatory authority, stakeholders, and even the auditee.

Each stakeholder has a different expectation regarding the audit. However, these extra personnel on the audit cannot be in the position to influence or otherwise interfere or prejudice the planning, conducting, and reporting the audit.

These extra people on the audit cannot be in a position to conflict or provide the appearance of a conflict of interest during the audit.

Some of these people may be restricted from different parts of the audit. Audit observers may have to be restricted from access to secure auditee areas with confidential and proprietary information.

As well, the auditee may provide personnel who serve as guides. These personnel may be responsible for obtaining audit information, interpreting material, securing Information Technology resources, and other audit activities to support the audit team and act on requests from the audit team lead.

Audit guides may be responsible for the following:

a. **Auditor assistance**
   Assisting the audit team lead and team members in identifying people to interview and setting up appointments for the interview.

b. **Access assistance**
   Accessing specific locations, such as restricted facilities at the auditee's site. This may involve obtaining badges and audit identification materials.

c. **Complying with auditee rules**
   Communicating in a timely manner access, security, health, safety, environmental, and audit information to the audit team. If there are any risks to the audit team, then the auditee guide facilitates the response.

d. **Audit witness**
   Providing audit cooperation and if necessary witnessing the audit from the auditee's perspective.

e. **Information clarification**
   Providing audit assistance in setting up interviews, collecting

information, obtaining information, and clarification of audit points.

6.4.3 CONDUCTING OPENING MEETING

Each audit whether it is first-party, second-party, or third-party, starts with an opening meeting with the auditee. Audit team lead is responsible for setting up the agenda for the opening meeting.

The following may be involved in the opening meeting:

a. **Confirm agreement**
   Auditee, client, and audit team lead agree to the audit plan and audit report. Other interested parties may also be in attendance.

b. **Audit team introductions**
   Audit team members, observers, and technical experts are introduced to the auditee. Each audit team member roles and responsibilities are explained.

c. **Audit planning**
   Audit team discusses with the auditee that all scheduled audit activities should be conducted during the audit.

The audit team lead develops a plan for the opening meeting with auditee management. Audit senior management and personnel involved in the audit should attend the opening meeting. The opening meeting will cover programs, processes, functions, projects, and products that will be audited. Auditee has the opportunity to ask questions to clarify confusing points.

The opening meeting should have sufficient detail so that any potential misunderstandings that may arise are appropriately addressed.

The length and depth of the opening meeting should be based on the context of the organization. The opening meeting in a small organization may involve explaining the purpose of the audit, areas to be audited, and interview requirements.

In opening audit meetings, minutes should be taken and records of attendance can be retained. The audit team lead often chairs the meeting.

The audit team lead should consider the following in conducting the opening meeting:

- Identify all the participants, observers, technical experts, guides, and interpreters. Each person's responsibilities and roles should be covered.

- Identify specific audit tasks as well as the audit methods for conducting the audit.

- Identify specific activities to manage auditee risks will be covered.

During the opening meeting, the audit team lead should confirm with the auditee the following:

- Audit objectives, scope, and audit criteria.

- Audit plan and specific audit activities with the auditee. At a minimum, they can include date, schedule, resources required, and people and resources needed to conduct the audit. If there any changes that are anticipated, then these will be resolved during the audit.

- Formal communication channels between the auditee and the audit team.
- Audit language between the audit team and the auditee. If the audit language is not native of either the audit team or the auditee, then an interpreter will be assigned to the team.
- Auditor will keep the auditee informed of progress, issues, risks, or any material items during the audit.
- Auditee will provide resources, facilities, Information Technology, access, and any audit resources required by the audit team.
- Proprietary, confidential, secure, and classified information will be handled carefully. Auditee will provide access two areas that may be restricted. As well the auditee will provide health, safety, and environmental information as it regards to the audit scope and objectives.
- Auditor and auditee may discuss what audit team operations that may disrupt auditee's operations.

Following items may also be addressed during the opening meeting:

- Method, style, content, evidence, and technology for reporting conclusions and findings. It should be noted that some audit areas may be graded for example from A to F or 1 through 5 based on the importance of the finding.

- Under certain conditions audits may be restricted or even terminated. The conditions under which either may occur should be clarified during the audit meeting.

- Auditee may have some responsibilities regarding possible audit findings. The auditor may be in a position to write an explanation or even rebut audit findings.

- Auditor may have audit means to provide feedback to the audit team such as reviewing audit findings and providing additional information that may clarify some audit findings. As well, the team should have a process for complaints, escalation, or even appeal of the findings.

Commentary: Tailor and craft the opening meeting agenda to the context of the audit. More audit objectives would imply a more detailed opening meeting.

6.4.4 COMMUNICATING DURING THE AUDIT

Communications during the audit need to be formalized. Communication protocols can be developed among the audit team. Communication protocols are especially important when conducting a statutory or a regulatory audit. The auditee wants to make sure that it complies with requirements. Also, there might be mandatory reporting requirements in the statute.

The audit team lead can establish a daily or weekly meeting among team members to exchange audit information, ensure that audit objectives are being met, assess progress, and if necessary secure additional resources or assign members to new duties as needed.

The audit team lead can report progress on any material issues and problems to auditee and to the audit client. As well, there can be an escalation protocol developed for critical audit issues.

During the audit, additional issues may be discovered. Some of these issues may reveal material, chronic, systemic, or structural problems. These risks and problems should be reported to the auditee.

Important issues may be due to misunderstanding by team members of the auditee risks and controls. Or, the auditee may suggest alternate types of controls to mitigate these risks. However, it is critical that the audit team lead discusses these immediately with the auditee. Sometimes, the audit client may be notified of these risks. However, we recommend that the auditee is first informed and has a chance to resolve the issues prior to discussing these with the audit client.

Often these risks or concerns may be outside the scope of the audit. If such is the case, these should be reported to the audit team lead and possibly forwarded to the audit client for discussion and resolution.

Sometimes when conducting the audit, the audit team will discover that audit risk and issues are simply beyond the scope of the audit, data are not available; or the audit a team does not have the knowledge, skills, or abilities to reach not objective. When these are the case then the audit team lead should discuss the reasons with the audit client and the auditee. Possibly, additional resources may be provided to the audit team to conclude the audit. As much as possible, if there are many reasons for possibly not concluding an audit, they should be discussed during the planning phase of the audit.

When conducting an audit, changes may have to be made to the audit plan. The auditee and all the client can have a chance to review and possibly accept these changes. Scoping change may require additional resources which the audit client may have to improve.

6.4.5 AUDIT INFORMATION AVAILABILITY AND ACCESS

Methods depend on specific audit objectives, scope, resources, scheduling, criteria, location, duration, suitability, assurance, and other factors. As much as possible, audit methods in the prior factors should be defined in the audit plan. Location of the audit is especially critical because the audit may be close to the auditee or it could be off shore. Offshore audits require more time to conduct as well as an interpreter or technical specialist.

Access to information, data, and evidence are critical in any audit. Information forms the backbone of the audit in terms of providing evidence to support a finding or critical decision. The critical questions to ask and determine regarding information availability should focus on the following: why, how, when, where, and who has the information. Most of these issues are independent of where the information was created, used, or stored.

Auditors have a variety of methods by which they can choose to gather information: interviewing, analyzing, securing, testing, and other methods. It is incumbent on the auditor to determine what is the correct and suitable method to secure the required information.

Commentary: Access to auditee information related to each audit objective is essential to completing the audit.

6.4.6 REVIEWING DOCUMENTED INFORMATION WHILE CONDUCTING THE AUDIT

Another critical activity of the audit team is to review documented information that relates to a specific audit objective. Auditor has several options in regards to evaluating documented information. The auditor can:

- Determine if the Management System conforms to a standard and audit criteria.
- Obtain information or data to support the finding regarding a specific objective.

The auditor may decide to review of audit information at different stages of the audit. For example, an auditor may conduct a desk review of the information prior to the audit and even during the planning phase. The auditor may conduct a review during the report reporting phase.

Audit team lead should list all the documented information relating to each audit objective. The audit team lead shares this with the auditee to ensure the information is available from the auditee. Sometimes, the auditee cannot provide the information required to satisfy a specific audit objective. In such cases, the auditor can work with the auditee to provide additional information or obtain secondary information related to satisfying audit objective and criteria. In some cases, the audit may be discontinued or suspended until the requisite information can be found.

6.4.7 COLLECTING AND VERIFYING INFORMATION

Auditor while conducting the audit will collect information relating to complex processes, projects, functions, and activities but may require a higher level of assurance. A higher level of assurance may require sampling and verifying a large population of items.

Critical element of ISO 19011:2018 is that evidence to support an objective may have to be verified. There are a number of methods to determine verification and validation. The degree of verification may depend on the auditor's professional judgment and exercise of due care. However for high-risk audit objectives, the degree of reliance that can be placed in the evidence may have to be higher than just simply an exercise of professional judgement. In such cases, the auditor may have to sample a population of items, interview additional people, or validate and verify the information in another manner.

Auditor will gather audit evidence to support a determination of a finding regarding an objective. The auditor should record the evaluation of the evidence. This forms the basis for an audit trail or audit decision. As discussed, the audit trail is significant because an independent third-party will be able to evaluate the evidence and hopefully arrive at a similar conclusion as the auditor did. So, the auditor must capture and retain all significant evidence in the working papers of the audit.

If during the conduct of the audit the auditor discovers there is additional evidence to support an audit decision, this should be reported to the audit team lead as well as reported in the audit papers. As well, the auditor may discover new risks and opportunities that relate to audit objectives, then these can be shared with the audit team lead.

The auditor needs to determine whether to share these with the auditee and or audit client.

An auditor has various methods to collect information relating to a specific audit objective:

- **Interviews**
  Auditee interviews are the most common method for securing audit information.
- **Observations**
  Observations of the auditee's operations provide real time information regarding audit objectives.
- **Analysis of data or documented information**
  Analysis of documentation specifically policies, procedures, and work instructions found in a manual is a well-used Management Systems method.

6.4.8 GENERATING AUDIT FINDINGS

The auditor gathers evidence regarding audit criteria which are mapped against an objective. Depending on the evidence, the auditor may determine whether there is a finding or not. Audit findings may indicate there is conformity in regard to audit criteria or a nonconformity. When there is nonconformity, the auditor will issue of finding.

ISO 19011:2018 allows the auditor to share conformity findings, good practices, opportunities for improvement, conclusions, and recommendations with the auditee.

If there are nonconformities which the supporting evidence indicates, the auditor should record these in the working papers. As well, the auditor may grade non-conformities depending on the context and risks to the organization. For example, a nonconformity can be quantitative or qualitative measures. Quantitative measures provide a grade of nonconformity from one to five. Qualitative measure may grade a nonconformity in terms of minor or severe.

At the end of the audit, the auditor may review the grading of the nonconformities with the auditee and the audit client. The auditee may want to have an agreement on the nature and level of risk of each grade. The auditor may want the auditee to review the grading to ensure there is agreement. The auditor wants to review the grading to ensure that there is sufficient evidence for an accurate and reliable finding.

The auditor may want to review the grading with the audit team to ensure that non-conformities are understood and possible corrective actions can jointly be determined. Finally, the auditor may want to discuss the non-conformities with the auditee to resolve any differences in opinions concerning findings, grading of findings, and the extent and type of evidence that was discovered to support the findings. Finally, unresolved issues may be recorded in the working papers or even the final audit report.

The audit team may meet daily or weekly to review audit findings and supporting evidence. If additional evidence is needed to support a finding, then additional resources or time should be allocated.

Commentary: Sufficient and accurate evidence needs to gathered related to each audit objective so an opinion can be rendered by the auditor. This is the basis for the auditor's due professional care.

6.4.9 DETERMINING AUDIT CONCLUSIONS

6.4.9.1 PREPARATION FOR CLOSING MEETING

The closing meeting is the final meeting with the auditee. Each audit should have a closing meeting. The purpose of the closing meeting with the auditee is to present the findings in the report, specifically:

a. **Auditing findings review**
   Review findings, recommendations, and opportunities for improvement with the auditee.
b. **Conclusion agreement**
   Share conclusions with the auditee and determine if there is agreement.
c. **Recommendations**
   Discuss any recommendations with the auditee. This should only be done if this was incorporated into the audit plan.
d. **Audit follow-up**
   Determine if any audit follow up is necessary regarding application of the findings.

6.4.9.2 CONTENT OF AUDIT CONCLUSIONS

Audit may report conclusions. Audit conclusions may address the following:

a. **Conformity with audit criteria**
   Discussion of the conformity of the findings regarding criteria;

effectiveness of the Management System; identification of risks: effectiveness of auditee actions to mitigate the risks; and efficiency, effectiveness, and economics of management controls.

b. **Effective implementation**
   Effective, efficient, and economic design, deployment, and improvement of the Management System.

c. **Audit objective achievement**
   Ability of the audit team to achieve the audit objectives within schedule, budget, scope, and quality.

d. **Joint audit findings**
   Determination of similar observations within the organization that may indicate possible areas for improvement or for trending analysis.

The auditor may have developed an audit plan with recommendations, risks, controls or other activities may be reported in the final report. However, they should have been discussed and negotiated with the auditee and the client prior to conducting the audit.

Commentary: A reminder: risk and opportunities should be considered in planning, conducting, and reporting the audit.

6.4.10 CONDUCTING CLOSING MEETING

Audit team lead is responsible for discussing preliminary audit findings and conclusions with the auditee in the final meeting. Customer, auditee, and auditor management and interested parties may attend the meeting.

The closing meeting may include the following:

- Auditee principles who are interviewed.
- Audit client.
- Auditee management.
- Audit team members, technical experts, and observers.

Audit stakeholders and other interested parties who have been invited by the audit client, audit manager, and auditee.

In the final meeting, the audit team lead can discuss events, circumstances, and other situations that may occurred during the audit that may increase or decrease the level of confidence in the audit results. If there are disagreements, then these should be resolved before the final meeting. As well, the key audit stakeholders should agree on a schedule and action plan for resolution of these issues.

During the closing meeting, the client, audit team lead, and audit team can develop a plan and a time frame to address audit findings.

The closing meeting should have an agenda. The audit team lead is responsible for developing the closing meeting agenda.

The amount of information shared during the closing meeting depends on the criticality of the audit findings related to specific audit objectives. The effectiveness, efficiency, and economics of the Management System in achieving the auditee's objectives or determining compliance to criteria can be considered in developing the closing meeting agenda. Another consideration may include organizational context, observed risks, and opportunities for improvement.

If the auditee is not familiar with the Management System audit process or ISO 19011:2018, then the audit team lead may spend additional time explaining the scope, context, objectives, risks, and opportunities of the audit. The amount of detail in the explanation can depend on the criticality audit and the context of the auditee.

The final closing meeting in most cases will be formal with an agenda and minutes. The minutes of the meeting may include people attended, purpose, discussion topics, disagreements, and possible resolution of disagreements. An audit meeting may be informal for example for an internal or first-party audit. Again, the level of detail depends on the context of the auditee.

A discussion of each audit objective should be discussed in the final meeting. If there are multiple objectives, each one should be covered in sequence with specific evidence as well as any findings that relate to each specific objective.

If the final meeting is not formal, then a set of discussion issues can be addressed in a closing meeting. However, the following criteria may be introduced in the closing meeting:

a. **Sample risks**
   If samples are taken to determine compliance or adherence, then an explanation of the audit evidence can be provided.

b. **Reporting method**
   Audit findings relating to the agreed-on audit process.

c. **Risks**
   Risks of not suitably addressing audit findings related to an objective. Audit findings, conclusions, risks, and opportunities

for improvement can be covered so the auditee fully understands audit results.

d. **Audit finding resolution**

If any post audit activities such as corrective actions, audit finding escalation, resolution, post evaluation review of control effectiveness, or anything else can be considered.

e. **Consequences of no corrective action**

ISO 9000 is risk-based and detailed in its requirements and recommendations. As a result, disagreements may result between the auditor and auditee. Disagreements can be discussed and resolved during the closing meeting. Sometimes, this cannot be done. In such cases, the auditor may have several options such as resolving the issues during the audit, escalating the findings for further discussion with a client or audit manager, developing post audit corrective actions, or even submitting a written rebuttal in the audit report.

f. **Positive recommendations**

Opportunities for improvement and positive recommendations may be presented in the final audit report. This is optional. However, they should have been negotiated prior to conducting the audit and can be part of the audit plan.

g. **Post audit activities**

ISO 19011:2018 states that recommendations, conclusions, and opportunities for improvement are not binding on the auditee.

6.5 PREPARING AND DISTRIBUTING THE AUDIT REPORT

6.5.1 PREPARING AUDIT REPORT

Audit team lead is responsible for architecting, preparing, organizing, and developing the final audit report. The audit report should provide a complete and accurate overview of the audit. This is commonly called an audit trail so that an independent third-party can reach the same conclusions and findings as the audit team. The audit team in the final report addressed each of the audit objectives and issues a finding relating to the audit criteria in that audit objective.

Each audit report follows a similar pattern however the specifics in the report reflects the audit objectives.

The final audit report can include:

a. **Audit objectives**
   Identify objectives of the audit.

b. **Audit scope**
   Scope the audit including processes, programs, projects, products, transactions, services, and other functions that were audited.

c. **Audit client**
   Identify audit client, stakeholders, and interested parties.

d. **Audit team identification**
   Identify audit team members.

e. **Audit dates**
   Identify location, schedule, and dates of the audit.

f. **Audit criteria**
Identify audit criteria for each audit objective.

g. **Audit findings**
Link audit findings directly to audit criteria and an objective. Evidence to support the finding may be added.

h. **Audit conclusions**

Provide audit conclusions based on findings.

i. **Degree of adherence**
Determine degree of adherence against criteria.

j. **Difference in opinion**
Resolve differences in opinion between audit team and auditee. Issues may be unresolved during the audit. Unresolved issues may include diverging opinions, insufficient evidence, unavailable people to be interviewed, and other issues.

k. **Audit risks**
Identify audit risks. Audits are based on the exercise of due professional care and due diligence by the audit team. However, there are always risks that insufficient audit evidence may be available, insufficient interviews were conducted, and other issues. These are the risks that may or may not be discussed during the audit.

Final audit report may include the following:

- **Audit plan.**
  Description of the audit objectives, criteria, methods, and findings.

- Description of the audit process and methods relating to each of the audit objectives. Any risks or hindrances that may have been uncovered during the audit may be addressed.

- Description of the audit objectives and audit criteria that were reviewed during planning and reporting the audit.

- Scope of the audit as well as any peripheral areas that may have been covered as a result of the audit. Areas that may or may have not been in the original audit plan are identified. Any areas that were in the audit plan dealing with audit scope that were not addressed may be listed.

- List of the audit conclusions, recommendations, and critical audit findings again specific objectives.

- List of best practices the team uncovered. This is often optional since the audit is based on a specific scope and objectives.

- If there are any findings, then the auditee, audit client, and laid made negotiate a follow-up on specific findings.

- Discussion of confidentiality, and information integrity. If the team used any proprietary, confidential, or secret information, then there can be a statement that this information will only be retained and secured facilities for this amount of time.

- Subsequent audits with specific findings or follow up audits may be discussed.

6.5.2 DISTRIBUTING THE AUDIT REPORT

The audit report is conducted to provide information or assurance to the audit client. The audit may be time constrained where the audit may be needed for some type of problem solving or decision-making. So, the audit team lead is responsible for issuing the audit report within the agreed and negotiated time. If the audit report cannot be delivered on time, then the reasons for the delay should be communicated to the auditee, client, audit manager, and other stakeholders who rely on the audit report information.

The audit team lead is responsible for ensuring that report is distributed to the client and other parties. Audit team lead is responsible for dating, reviewing, and approving the final report. Audit manager may review the final report and approve it.

Many organizations have an audit distribution list. The audit team lead is responsible for ensuring that each of these persons receives the audit report.

The audit team lead is responsible for securing proprietary, confidential, and secret information.

6.6 COMPLETING THE AUDIT

The audit is formally ended when all the planned audit asks have been completed, the audit client and audit team lead negotiate scoping the audits or even ending it prematurely.

The audit team must compile documented information and evidence obtained during an audit into a file. These are called working papers.

Depending on audit requirements, audit papers may have to be retained for a specified by rules or statute. Also, proprietary, confidential, sensitive, and classified information may have requirements for their destruction.

The audit team lead can ensure that there are any restrictions to the disclosure or dissemination of the audit information. Some audits are classified and confidential. Some may be in the public domain. Some audits may have non-disclosure requirements.

The audit manager and lead can determine disclosure requirements for each specific audit and potentially each audit objective. If disclosure of a confidential audit is required by legal action, the audit team lead informs the client and auditee.

Each audit offers opportunities for improvement and lessons learned. These lessons learned can be captured and discussed throughout the audit organization.

6.7 CONDUCTING THE FOLLOW-UP AUDIT

Sometimes, an audit will result in findings that require subsequent validation or verification that audit recommendations were implemented. Recommendations may involve corrective actions, opportunities for improvement, compliance, or other Management System applications.

The audit team lead, audit client, and auditee discuss subsequent audit review during the closing phase of the audit. The client and auditee may agree on a time frame for application or correction, then a subsequent follow-up by the audit team. As well the audit team lead can communicate these new requirements to the audit manager and keep the audit team apprised of any follow-up. The effectiveness, efficiency, and economics of a follow-up may have to be verified and validated. And such cases, a detailed or simple verification may be conducted on specific objectives. The lead auditor can report the subsequent review or verification to the audit manager and to the client.

7 COMPETENCE AND EVALUATION OF AUDITORS

7.1 GENERAL

The competence of auditors is critical to maintain the credibility of the audit program. Auditors are critical for organizational governance, risk management, and compliance, the effectiveness, efficiency, and economics of an audit. Ultimately, auditors provide confidence to the client that the auditee's controls are in place, auditee is meeting its objectives, and auditee is in compliance.

Audit team lead and audit team competence are critical to the audit process and audit findings. Competence of the audit team lead and team can be evaluated through their knowledge, skills, abilities, and behavior during the audit. Other factors to evaluate in terms auditor competence include education, work experience, training, certifications, and experience.

Process of evaluating auditor competence should be determined during auditor selection, training, professional development, and promotion.

Audit team may be composed of auditors of different skill levels and technical abilities. The critical issue is that competence of the overall audit team should be sufficient to plan, conduct, and report the audit results.

The audit manager and or the audit team lead should have a process for evaluating each auditor based on objective criteria. The evaluation process may involve the following steps:

a. **Auditor competence**
   Work and professional description of the job requirements to be a professional auditor.

b. **Auditor evaluation criteria**
   Description and evaluation criteria for due professional care.

c. **Auditor evaluation method**
   Development of an auditor, audit team lead, and technical expert process.

d. **Conduct the auditor evaluation**
   Process to determine how to evaluate auditor competence.

Once the evaluation process is finished, the audit manager or audit team lead can:

- Select audit team members based on knowledge, skills, and abilities.
- Determine gaps in knowledge, skills, and abilities and determine how to close these gaps.
- Conduct evaluation of individual auditors based on professional development and skills applied during the audit.

More companies are requiring auditors to continually identify potential gaps and their competence and continually improve. Some companies call this self-management. The purpose is to see the potential for continual improvement.

ISO 19011:2018 describes a process for:

- Evaluating audit team leads and team members.
- Identifying the criteria by which performance can be evaluated.
- Identifying the competence level required of Management System Auditors.

Commentary: ISO 19011:2018 sets a higher level of professional care when planning, reporting, and conducting an audit. Auditors and leads need to be extensively trained and evaluated for the new standard.

7.2 DETERMINING AUDITOR COMPETENCE

7.2.1 General

Reliance and trust in an audit is based on the credibility of the audit team lead and audit team. In determining auditor competence for an audit, the audit manager and audit team lead can evaluate auditor knowledge, skills, and abilities based on the following criteria:

a. **Auditee's context**
   Type, complexity, objective, and criteria of the auditee's programs, projects, processes, products, services and functions being audited.

b. **Auditing methods**
   Auditing methods. More complex methods require a higher level of confidence.

c. **Management disciplines audited**
Management Systems being audited and audit objectives. For example, a compliance audit of statutory requirements is different than a Management System audit.

d. **Management Systems complexity**
Objectives and Management Systems being audited.

e. **Auditee risks and opportunities**
Types and consequences faced in conducting the audit.

f. **Audit program objectives**
Goals and objectives of the overall audit program.

g. **Audit objective uncertainty**
Ambiguity and volatility in the auditee to achieve audit objectives.

h. **Additional requirements**
Additional requirements may be imposed by the client or audit stakeholders.

7.2.2 PERSONAL BEHAVIOR

The credibility of an audit report is determined by auditor's due professional care. Part of this concept is the auditor's personal behavior when planning, conducting, and reporting the audit.

Auditors can follow the principles as outlined in ISO 19011:2018. These principles describe the requisite professional and personal behavior of auditors.

While there is no set of approved behaviors of Management System auditors, the following is a list of common attributes:

a. **Ethics**
Auditor exhibits ethical behavior when planning, conducting, and reporting the audit. Ethical behavior may involve discretion, fairness, objectivity, and Independence.

b. **Open minded**
Auditor is open to different points of view as well as considering different types of evidence to arrive at a conclusion regarding a finding or compliance.

c. **Tactful**
Auditor recognizes that the auditee's workplace and culture may have some specific rules and the auditor is cognizant of these.

d. **Observant**
Auditor has the capacity to actively observe auditee conditions, surroundings, and.

e. **Sensitive**
Auditor has the ability to understand people, processes, and culture.

f. **Flexible**
Auditor can adapt to new cultures, environments, and organizations.

g. **Persistent**
Auditor is focused on planning, conducting, and reporting the audit.

h. **Resolute**
Auditor follows a logical and systematic process in conducting the audit and reaching conclusions and findings.

i. **Self-sustaining**
Auditor understands his or her audit responsibilities and conducts himself and herself in a professional manner.

j. **Resolute**
Auditor is independent, responsible, professional, and diligent.

k. **Continual learning**
Auditor is aware that each audit involves a new contract and is open to suggestions for improvement.

l. **Cultural awareness**
Auditor is aware the auditee's context and always conducts himself or herself in a professional manner.

m. **Co-operative**
Auditor can work with the members of the audit team and auditee's personnel.

7.2.3 KNOWLEDGE AND SKILLS

7 2.3.1 GENERAL

Auditor should have the following knowledge, skills, and abilities:

a. **Knowledge, skills and abilities**
Knowledge, skills, and abilities to plan, conduct, and report in a professional manner.

b. **Professionalism**
Professional competence, discipline, and sector-specific knowledge in auditing skills.

Audit team lead has the right professional, technical, people, and process knowledge, skills, and abilities to manage the audit team.

7.2.3.2 GENERIC KNOWLEDGE AND SKILLS OF MANAGEMENT SYSTEM AUDITORS

Auditors need to have the following knowledge, skills, and abilities:

a. **Audit principle knowledge**

Audit principles, systems, processes, methods, people, IT, and people skills to ensure that audits are planned, conducted, and reported in a professional manner. As well, the auditor is able to conduct these audits in a consistent and professional fashion so that independent third-party would arrive at the same conclusions as the audit team.

A competent auditor can:

- Define and identify risks and opportunities relating to planning, conducting, and reporting the audit. This is a key element for risk-based auditing.
- Plan, conduct, and report the audit results effectively, efficiently, and economically.
- Conduct the audit within the agreed-on schedule with the audit client and auditee.
- Prioritize the critical few items compared to the insignificant many in the audit.
- Communicate and report audit results effectively, efficiency, and economically. Communication may involve the written report as well as a verbal report.
- Gather data and information which become critical evidence through analysis, interviews, reviewing information, and through other means.

- Use appropriate and suitable techniques for gathering audit information such as article sampling, data analysis, and other methods.
- Plan, conduct, and report audit results in a professional manner.
- Understand various risks in the organization including whitespace risks, dependency risks, interdependency risks, and other critical risks.
- Validate IT information specifically related to audit objectives.
- Validate the suitability and appropriateness of audit information and evidence to support audit findings, conclusions, recommendations, opportunities for improvement, and other audit results.
- Determine the critical factors that impact the accuracy and verifiability of the audit findings, conclusions, and recommendations.
- Prepare audit papers so they provide a logic trail for each audit finding and audit objective.
- Ensure the confidentiality and security of all information obtained during the audit.

b. **Management system knowledge**

Management System standards such as ISO 9001:2015 and ISO 14001: 2015 contain specific criteria that are essential for understanding audit scope and audit objectives. Management System standards often include the following:

- Standard requirements such as 'shalls' that define specific criteria or methods.
- Design and deployment of the Management System standard by the auditee.
- Process interrelationships between and among Management System standards.
- Description of the critical compliance areas of multiple Management System standards or references.
- Specific requirements in application of the standards to specific situations.

c. **Auditee context knowledge**
Auditor in each Management System standard must be aware of the auditee's context. The auditor should have knowledge, skills, and abilities in the auditee's sector, business model, structure, and management practices.

The auditor should have knowledge, skills, and abilities in the following contextual areas:

- Specific requirements of an audit client.
- Governance, risk management, compliance, structure, size, business model, and functions of the auditee.
- Business model used in the Management System, processes, technology, people, and Information Technology of the auditee.
- Environmental, social, cultural, and other contextual issue related to the auditee.

d. **Statutory and regulatory knowledge**
The auditor may be working in a statutory and regulatory environment. These audits are often compliance to specific requirements. The auditor needs to have knowledge, skills, and abilities related to specific statutory and regulatory requirements in order to plan, conduct, and report audit results. The auditor should also information regarding the audit.

- Statutory or regulatory regular work knowledge.
- Fundamental business law understanding.
- Contracting and legal taxonomy understanding.

7.2.3.3 DISCIPLINE AND SECTOR-SPECIFIC COMPETENCE OF AUDITORS

Depending on audit requirements, the audit team may be composed of one or more people. The audit team whether it is one person or multiple persons should have the requisite competence and collective knowledge to plan, conduct, and report audit results.

The audit team should have sector-specific abilities and discipline to plan conduct the audit, specifically:

a. **Management System knowledge**
Understanding of the Management System requirements, principles, and processes.

b. **Auditee discipline knowledge**
Understanding of the Management System standards that are being used by the auditee.

c. **Application knowledge**
Understanding of the sector specific tools, techniques, and

best practices to plan, conduct, and report results against specific criteria.

d. **Risk and opportunities knowledge**
   Understanding of how to evaluate risks and opportunities related to the audit objectives. The auditor needs to understand the principles, processes, at techniques that are specific to the auditee's discipline in order to evaluate the risks for planning, conducting, and reporting audit results.

Commentary: More sectors are adding their own requirements on top of ISO 9001:2015 and other standards. Auditors need this additional sector-specific knowledge, skills, and abilities to conduct audits.

7.2.3.4 GENERIC COMPETENCE OF TEAM LEADER

The audit team lead is responsible for managing the audit effectively, efficiently, and economically. The audit team lead should have knowledge, skills, and abilities to:

a. **Plan audit**
   Plan the audit so that the objective has specific criteria to be met, and all the tasks that are necessary for evaluating evidence against the criteria and issuing a finding are identified.

b. **Strategic perspective**
   Discuss business, strategic, and tactical issues with auditee management to evaluate whether these issues have been discussed in terms of risks and opportunities.

c. **Cooperative environment**
   Promote a cooperative relationship among audit team members.

d. **Ability to manage**
Manage the entire audit process, including planning, conducting, and reporting. As well, the audit team lead is responsible for the following:

- Using audit resources including personnel, equipment, Information Technology, and money's effectively, efficiently, and economically.
- Managing the uncertainty that is inherent in any audit so that audit objectives can be reached.
- Ensuring the safety of team members. Safety may involve protective clothing, safety gear, and other actions. As well, the team lead must understand and be able to comply with the auditee's environmental, security, health, safety, and other organizational compliance issues.
- Managing audit team members to complete the audit on time and within budget.
- Mentor and provide direction to auditors in training.
- Prevent conflicts and resolve issues that may arise during the planning, conducting, and reporting of the audit.

e. **Communication abilities**
Represent the audit team in communications with audit program manager, audit stakeholders, audit interested parties, and other relevant parties.

f. **Lead audit team**
Ensure the audit team completes the audit within schedule and meets its audit objectives.

g. Complete audit report

Complete the audit report and ensure that audit papers address each of the audit objectives.

7.2.3.5 KNOWLEDGE AND SKILLS OF AUDITING MULTIPLE DISCIPLINES

As a whole, the audit team should have the requisite knowledge, skills, and abilities to plan, conduct, and report each of the Management Systems as well as its requirements.

Each Management System has 'shall' requirements, risk and opportunity requirements, and compliance objectives. The audit team lead should be able to understand and identify the requirements of each Management System standard and recognize what is required to determine compliance or effectiveness for each requirement.

7.2.4 ACHIEVING AUDITOR COMPETENCE

Audit team including audit team lead and members should be competent to plan, conduct, and report audit results. Auditor competence may involve the following:

a. Training completion

Completing an audit team lead, auditor, and audit training programs. Auditor training is becoming an essential element for determining auditor competency and auditor due diligence.

b. Relevant experience

Demonstrated experience in conducting a Management System audit. As well, the auditor should have suitable professional and technical and sector-specific expertise in each Management System. The auditor should have problem solving and decision-making capabilities in order to plan, conduct, and report audit results to audit stakeholders.

c. **Education and training**

Specific training and experience in each Management System that is being audited. As well, more often sector-specific requirements are being developed so an auditor should have knowledge and experience in these.

d. **Audit experience**

Audit experience can be under the supervision of an audit team lead that has specific knowledge skills and abilities in the specific discipline in Management System.

7.2.5 ACHIEVING AUDIT TEAM LEAD COMPETENCE

Audit team lead manages the entire audit from planning, conducting to reporting audit results. The audit team lead can have gained experience under the guidance of a different audit team lead or manager. In a small company, the lead may be the only auditor of a Management System. This person becomes the program manager, audit team lead, and auditor.

7.3 ESTABLISHING AUDITOR EVALUATION CRITERIA

Organization should have established criteria for becoming an auditor. The criteria may include knowledge, skills, and abilities to plan, conduct, and report the audit. Auditor criteria should include desired audit behaviors. Another area may include quantitative and qualitative criteria. Quantitative includes years of experience and audit training. Qualitative criteria includes peer reviews, mentoring, and peer guidance.

7.4 SELECTING APPROPRIATE AUDITOR EVALUATION METHOD

Auditors can be evaluated by a number of methods. ISO 19011:2018 has a very detailed table providing information on conducting an auditor evaluation. ISO 19011:2018 suggests that an auditor can be evaluated using two or more of the methods that are listed below:

a. **Audit methods**

   Selection and evaluation methods of auditors can be applied to the context of the organization.

b. **Audit accuracy**

   Methods for selecting and evaluating an auditor should be based on the context of the organization and may differ in terms of the reliability.

c. **Selection of appropriate methods**

   Combination of methods for selecting and evaluating auditors should provide consistent outcomes regarding the suitability and professionalism of the auditor.

7.5 CONDUCTING AUDITOR EVALUATION

An organization should have a selection and evaluation method for Management System auditors. The organization can define the criteria against which auditors are going to be evaluated. If auditor does not or cannot meet the criteria then the organization has the option to provide additional training, guidance, mentoring, experience, or subsequent reevaluation.

7.6 MAINTAINING AND IMPROVING AUDITOR COMPETENCE

The auditing organization should strive for continual improvement of its audit process, methods, techniques, and auditor skills. Maintaining auditor competence is part of an overall auditing continual improvement program.

Audit team lead and auditors can maintain their auditing competence by being actively involved in planning, conducting, and reporting audits. This is part of an overall professional development program. As well, auditor competence can be enhanced through additional training, mentoring, seminars, and other techniques.

The audit manager is responsible for establishing a suitable program for the continual selection, evaluation, and improvement of the audit program. A critical element is continual improvement of the professional development of the audit team leads and audit team members.

Auditor professional development may address the following:

a. **Organizational changes**
   Organizations are being disrupted. In the context of the auditing organization, auditors must know what to expect if its auditing organization is changing.

b. **Technology changes**
   Changes in the audit team leads and auditors.

c. **Standard changes**
   Recognition of best practices including use of new technologies.

d. **Auditing discipline changes**
   New standards for planning, conducting, and reporting audits. specific sector requirements and changes in technology.

ANNEX A: INFORMATIVE

Annex A is informative providing guidance to auditors in planning, conducting, and reporting audits. The guidance is not a specific requirement of the standard.

ISO standards have specific requirements. If the standard has an Annex then it generally provides additional description, context, guidance, and information on a specific topic of the standard. These Annexes tend to be optional. However, they are very useful for filling in the blanks in many ISO standards that sometimes are descriptive rather than prescriptive. In such cases, the Annex provides additional information and often best practices in a particular subject area of the standard.

8.1 APPLYING AUDIT METHODS

The auditor can use a number of techniques, methods, skills, and tools for planning, conducting, and reporting the audit. The specific tool or process the auditor uses is largely based on the context of client organization requesting the audit, the auditing organization, and the organization being audited.

For example, the client organization requesting the audit may require a higher level of confidence or assurance. The client may have the audit conducted within a specific time frame and define specific audit criteria. The audit organization may not have auditors with specific skills knowledge required. Or, the auditee may have specific technology or proprietary systems that may require a non-disclosure agreement.

So, the critical point is that depending a number of factors may have to be optimized from the audit client, auditing organization, and auditee. Audit methods, audit criteria, audit objective, scope, duration, location, people, Information Technology, processes, and many other details have to be decided before the audit is scoped. As well auditor competence and other uncertainties may dictate the type of audit methods that must be applied.

The audit team lead after consultation with the client may have to determine the optimal methods and tools to be used so the audit is effective, efficient, and economic.

ISO 19011:2018 offers much guidance on audit performance and methods. Audit performance may include: auditor capabilities, due diligence, training, expertise, common knowledge, skills, and abilities.

As well, there are soft skills to consider in audit performance such as the ability of the auditor to communicate, coordinate, cooperate, obtain the requisite information from the audit and many other social factors and behaviors.

The auditor is responsible for determining the appropriate audit methods and their application. The audit team lead defines these in the planning stage of the audit. ISO 19011:2018 mentions that the program manager may be involved in audit method selection.

Remote auditing is one of the approved methods. Remote auditing means much of the audit is done off site, specifically away from the auditee's main place of business. An example of remote auditing might be a desk audit reviewing auditee's policies, procedures, and work instructions off site. The effectiveness of remote auditing depends on a number of factors, specifically being able to achieve audit objectives, ability to gather the requisite level and kind of evidence, being able to interview the auditee and regulatory requirements.

At the audit program level, the audit manager or the audit team lead determines if a remote application of audit methods is suitable. In some case the level of assurance or competence is determined by the audit client, the audit manager, audit team lead, or even auditee's management.

Commentary: Audit method(s) needs to be tailored to the audit objective.

A.2 PROCESS APPROACH TO AUDITING

Process approach is now a fundamental element in ISO 9001:2015. The process approach now is a requirement for all ISO Management System standards.

Auditors must know how to conduct their audits using a process approach. The process approach follows resources, decisions, products, and services from beginning to end. As well, the auditor needs to look at the interactions among interacting processes in a Management System. This way, if all the auditors follow a consistent and linear approach to conducting audits, then the results should be predictable from one auditor to another.

Commentary: Many Management System auditors do not know how to conduct a process audit - even though it has been a requirement since 2000.

A.3 PROFESSIONAL JUDGEMENT

More Management System standards focus on processes and outcomes. An auditor may not have a 'shall' requirement. So, Management System auditor needs to use his or her professional judgment when evaluating generic requirements in a Management System standard.

An auditor in previous Management System standards conducted a compliance assessment. The auditor determined if manual, policies, procedures, and work instructions adhered to 'shall' requirements in the standard.

The challenge is that new Quality Management standards do not lend themselves to reviewing compliance documents. The auditor has to apply his or her professional judgment to the context, content, audit criteria, and audit objectives.

Commentary: Professional judgement is the key to successful ISO 19011:2018 audits since more Management System requirements are open to auditor and auditee interpretation.

A.4 PERFORMANCE RESULTS

Auditor needs to be more focused on the intended outcome of the Management System throughout the audit. 'Shall' requirements are still important. Processes are still important. But now, auditors need to focus on the outcomes of the Management System as well as its performance. Performance can be defined in terms of the Management Systems effectiveness, efficiency, and economics.

Manuals or similar documentation were normally a requirement for passing a clause-by-clause compliance audit. Now, Management System standards allow the auditee to use audit evidence and documentation as evidence to demonstrate implementation of the Management System.

Context is an important new concept and ISO standards. For example, ISO 19011:2018 states that this might not be as important in a smaller organization as a larger complex organization.

A.5 VERIFYING INFORMATION

A challenge that an auditor may face is securing sufficient information to confirm that 'shall' requirements are being met or the audit objective can be satisfied.

Auditor, as much as possible, can:

a. **Complete information**
   Obtain complete and objective information that supports the audit objective.

b. **Accurate information**
   Ensure audit information is reliable and accurate.

c. **Standard information**
   Ensure audit information is similar to audit related documents and evidence.

d. **Up to date information**
   Ensure audit information and evidence is up to date.

The auditor should consider that information relates directly to an audit requirement and demonstrates that a requirement is being met.

Sometimes information and evidence related to an audit objective is in a different form, extent, media, or other unexpected matter. The such cases, the auditor should gather sufficient evidence to ensure that the audit objective is being met.

Information security is now a critical part of ISO 19011:2018. Information security may be subject to regulations and requirements, which require specific protection or security. It is critical that the audit team lead understands the applicable requirements and complies during the audit.

A.6 SAMPLING

A.6.1 GENERAL

In a large population of items, the auditor may decide to take a sample from the population because it is not necessary or too expensive to examine the entire population of items. Upon sampling, the auditor must choose a random, representative, and statistically valid sample of the entire population. The purpose of the sample is to make a determination about the larger population of similar items.

The auditor will sample the population of items regarding a specific audit objective. The sample will be used to determine if the audit objective has been achieved. The sample will provide a level of confidence to the auditor regarding compliance.

There are risks in sampling. A common risk is that the samples may not be representative of the population of items. The result is the auditors finding may be biased and have a lower level of confidence that is required by the audit client. Another risk is there might be inherent variability within the population. Also, the auditor may choose a method of sampling that is incorrect.

To ensure sampling confidence, the auditor often employs the following steps in conducting sampling:

a. **Sampling goal**
   Determine specific sampling objectives.
b. **Population**
   Determine the size, composition, of the population of items to be sampled.

c. **Sampling method**
   Determine the appropriate method for sampling.

d. **Sample size**
   Determine the sample size to be reviewed.

e. **Sampling method**
   Collect a sample from the population.

f. **Sampling results**
   Review each sample item according to the requirements of the audit test, and then document the results.

The auditor when sampling should consider the quality of the data and the suitability of the sampling method. Data may be inaccurate or not available. Or, the auditor is not familiar with the population of items or uses an incorrect sampling method.

Once completed, the auditor can report in the working papers the population of items, sample selected, sampling standard, method of sampling, sample size, confidence level, and other significant criteria.

The auditor may want to use a statistical sampling method or a professional judgement based sampling method. Both are acceptable. However, the reason for choosing the sampling method should be noted in the working papers.

A.6.2 JUDGEMENT BASED SAMPLING

The auditor may use judgement based sampling depending on the auditor's competence, experience, knowledge, and professional due diligence.

The following should be considered in determining whether judgement based sampling is used:

a. **Sampling experience**
   Previous experience sampling similar populations of items.

b. **Sampling regulatory requirements**
   Regulatory or statutory requirements may require a specific type of sampling related to a specific audit objective.

c. **Auditee's complexity**
   Consistency of the population of items to be sampled and the complexity of the process that generated the population of items.

d. **Changes in sampling factors**
   Information Technology, security, human factors, or process requirements population.

e. **Risks and opportunities**
   Review of the risks and opportunities of using judgment based sampling.

f. **Management System monitoring**
   Results from reviewing the Management System.

Judgment sampling is largely effective if the auditor has sufficient experience to make assurance and quality decisions. The effectiveness of judgment a sampling is based on professional abilities and judgment of the auditor. However, judgement based sampling does not provide a statistical estimate or the competence level of the result.

A.6.3 STATISTICAL SAMPLING

The auditor can use statistical sampling to determine if an objective has been met. The auditor needs to understand the characteristics of the overall population of items. If the population of items is not consistent or is non-homogeneous, then statistical sampling becomes more difficult. The auditor then needs to ensure that the sample that is selected is representative of the entire population of items that are being evaluated.

The auditor needs to develop a statistical sampling plan. This requires more knowledge of probability and statistics. One common statistical plan is based on attributes. The auditor will select a sample and evaluate each product based on a specific characteristic or attribute. The auditor then determines if the sample selected does have that attribute or does not. This is basically a binary decision involving pass or fail. Another option is to use variable sampling which is based on a series of results over the continuous range.

The auditor will design the sampling plan based on the audit objective. The plan can be attribute or variable based. For example, the auditor would then evaluate the sample for conformity to a requirement using an attribute based approach. The auditor would design a variable based approach if the auditor were evaluating a range of items such as the severity of an injury or the severity of a security breach.

The auditor can consider the following and designing a sampling plan:

a. **Auditee's context**
   Context, nature, complexity, regulations, requirements, materiality, or significance of the item being evaluated.

b. **Auditor size**
   Competency of the auditor in terms of statistical knowledge, skills, and abilities.

c. **Audit frequency**
   Frequency of the assessment or audit.

d. **Audit timing**
   Scheduling of the audit or assessment.

e. **Sample confidence**
   Required competence level by the client.

f. **Event occurrence**
   Possibility of uncertain events or factors.

The auditor using a statistical sampling plan will determine a level of sampling risk that the auditor is willing to accept. This is called the acceptable confidence level. A 95% confidence level implies a sampling risk of 5%. In this case, the auditor is willing to accept a risk that one in 20 samples will not reflect the entire population of items.

The auditor using a statistical sampling should document the process followed. The auditor should address each of the above elements.

Commentary: Know when or when not to sample. This key decision should be prominent in your work papers.

A.7 AUDITING COMPLIANCE WITHIN A MANAGEMENT SYSTEM

The auditor should consider the following when conducting the audit:

a. **Statutory compliance**
   Identify any statutory or regulatory requirements that must be met.

b. **Manage activities**
   Manage the projects, processes, activities, that result in products services that comply with these requirements.

c. **Compliance evaluation**
   Determine compliance or non-compliance to the statutory requirements.

The auditor may review or audit for compliance if the auditee:

1. **Change management process**
   Has a monitoring process to determine if there are changes to statutory or regulatory requirements and determine if an audit update needs to be considered.

2. **Compliance management**
   Has suitable professionals to manage and monitor compliance processes.

3. **Documented information**
   Reports on the status of the compliance program as well as current level of compliance regarding statutory and regulatory requirements.

4. **Internal audit program**
   Reviews the internal audit program for compliance.

5. **Non-compliance management**
   Corrects any non-compliances efficiently, effectively, and economically.

6. **Management reviews**
   Reports on compliance Management System reviews.

Commentary: Compliance is usually a simpler audit decision than an effectiveness audit decision. Understand how much evidence to gather to make a compliance audit decision.

A.8 AUDITING CONTEXT

New Management System standards require an organization to identify its context including the requirements and needs of clients, stakeholders, and interested parties.

An organization must use the concept of context in its strategic analysis and planning. An organization has two types of context: internal and external.

The auditor should be aware of these requirements in the new Management System standards. The auditor should first determine if context has been included in the Management System standard being audited. If it has, the auditor should review the auditee's definition and scope of context, both internal and external.

Auditor should evaluate if the auditee has suitably defined its context. The auditor will use the auditee's definition of context to determine the scope of the audit specifically relating to a Management System.

The auditor should collect evidence and data relating to context, specifically:

a. **Auditee's context methods**
   Review process used to determine internal and external context.

b. **Auditee's contextual competenc**e
   Review the knowledge, skills, and abilities of the people defining context.

c. **Auditee's contextual evaluation**
   Review the results of the process to define context.

d. **Management System application**
   Review how the organization has applied the process to define context.

e. **Context review**
   Review the application of the results from the previous step to determine the scope of the Management System and its development.

Monitoring the definition and application of auditee's definition of context is critical in conducting an audit of the new Management System standards. Auditors should have appropriate and sector specific knowledge, skills, and abilities to understand the auditee's definition of context and use of the concept of context in defining the scope of their Management System. The auditor then should make a reasonable and informed judgment as to the effectiveness the auditee uses to determine its context and scope of its Management System.

A.9 AUDITING LEADERSHIP AND COMMITMENT

New Management System standards focus on the importance of top management and leadership engagement.

Top management should demonstrate commitment, leadership, accountability, and responsibility for the effectiveness, efficiency, and effectiveness of its Management System. Management leadership ensures that the Management System is applied effectively. Top management activities and critical responsibilities can then be identified. As well, top management responsibilities that have been delegated should be identified.

Auditors must then be able to obtain objective evidence demonstrating that top management is involved in the decision-making relating to the Management System and how it demonstrates its commitment should be identified. The auditor can evaluate management commitment by reviewing organizational plans, strategic plan, policies, goals, objectives, resources, and external communications.

Auditors should interview top management to confirm they understand Management System requirements, context, and significant organizational issues. The auditor can then ensure that the Management System is working effectively, efficiently, and economically. Also, the auditor needs to have sufficient evidence that the Management System is achieving its intended objectives.

The auditor can evaluate top management but audit team leadership and commitment at different levels of the organization.

A.10 AUDITING RISKS AND OPPORTUNITIES

ISO Management System standards include the management of an organization risks and opportunities. So, auditors will now have an audit objective to evaluate and gather evidence regarding how the auditee manages its risks and opportunities.

An audit objective evaluating and gathering evidence for an organization's opportunities may include the following:

- Provide assurance on the reliability, accuracy and framework of the auditee's risk and opportunities identification process.
- Provide assurance that the identified risks and opportunities are adequately mitigated.
- Determine that the auditee addresses its risks and opportunities throughout the lifecycle of a project.

As mentioned, more Management System standards have risks and opportunities as requirements. The auditor, whether it is first-party, second-party, or third-party audit will now have to review the auditee's approach to mitigating its risks and going after opportunities.

ISO 19011:2018 recommends that auditor reviews risks and opportunities in every audit. Specifically, ISO 19011:2018 does not recommend that the risks and opportunities evaluation is conducted separately or as a separate evaluation or audit.

Risks and opportunities now are both explicit and implicit throughout planning, conducting, and reporting the audit including when interviewing top management.

The auditor should consider the following when gathering evidence of the auditee's risks and opportunities:

a. **Risk input review**
   Review the inputs used by the audit team to determine its risks in opportunities, including:

   - Analyzing contextual issues both internal and external.
   - Auditee's business model and strategic direction.
   - Auditee's stakeholders, clients, and interested parties specifically related to the Management System being audited.
   - External contextual risks such as safety, environmental, climate, geographic, and others.

b. **Risk sources**
   Evaluate the approaches for evaluating risks and opportunities may differ across sectors, functions, products, projects, and products.

The auditor will have to exercise due professional care to evaluate the auditee's control and management of its risks and opportunities. As well, the auditor will have to determine if the level of risk is appropriate to the organization and how it is and whether it is controlled effectively, efficiently, and economically.

Commentary: Auditing the auditee's risks and opportunity requirements is the biggest challenge in ISO 19011:2018. Why? The standard does now address Risk Based Thinking. The standard does not provide concrete examples of conducting risk audits.

A.11 LIFE CYCLE

New Management Systems are being developed that have a life cycle perspective and requirement for specific products and services. ISO 19011:2018 specifically states that auditors cannot consider this as a requirement to adopt a life cycle auditing approach with the auditee. The important point is that this is optional to the auditor.

Life cycle approach considers the identification, analysis, assessment, control, and mitigation of risks throughout the life cycle of a product or service.

Life cycle approach of an auditee may involve:

- Identifying market opportunities.
- Determining potential clients.
- Determining whether to provide the service or to outsource the service.
- Obtaining materials.
- Designing, producing, transporting the product to the client, and final disposal of the product.

Organizations received value using this approach in terms of owning life cycle, minimizing impact the environment, and adding value to clients. The auditor should use his or her professional judgment to determine whether cycle approach can be used in conducting the audit.

The auditor may consider the following factors in evaluating the auditee's life cycle approach:

a. **Lifecycle**
   Life cycle of the project, process, product, or service.

b. **Supply chain**
   Auditee's make or buy decision and its management of the supply chain.

c. **Supply chain length**
   Extent of the supply chain.

d. **Complexity**
   Programs, projects, products, and services have different or changing levels of complexity during their lifecycle. Complexity includes: technology, security, risk, process, product, or service being provided.

Organizations may have combined Management Systems to improve operational efficiency and effectiveness. In such cases, the auditor may have to evaluate intersecting life cycles of the Management Systems.

Commentary: Specify in your work papers, audit scope, or audit context whether you will be conducting a lifecycle audit.

A.12 AUDIT OF THE SUPPLY CHAIN

Organizations are outsourcing critical processes to key supply-partners. The auditor more often will have to evaluate auditee's supply chains. An audit of the auditee's supply chain may be added as a specific audit objective with criteria to be evaluated by the auditor.

The auditor may have to develop a plan for evaluating and auditing key suppliers as well as define audit criteria and scope of the supply chain audit.

A.13 PREPARING AUDIT WORK DOCUMENTS

Lead auditors need to develop specific work papers and documents regarding the audit. The purpose of work papers is to facilitate an independent third-party to follow the logic trail in the documents and reach the same conclusions on findings and recommendations as the audit team.

The auditor should consider the following in developing work papers, documents, and evidence to support each finding:

a. **Work papers list**
   Identify audit documents and evidence specifically related to a finding and audit objective.

b. **Audit documentation mapping**
   Link the audit document to the particular audit activity, including audit planning, conducting, and reporting.

c. **Document users**
   Identify the client of the work paper as well as its purpose in the audit.

d. **Work documentation preparation**
   Identify additional information that was used to evaluate the work documents and why it was important as evidence for determining a finding.

The auditor may be involved in combined audit where two or more audit teams evaluated audit documents. The auditor is responsible for ensuring that the auditee does not feel that their work is being disrupted. So, the auditor should avoid duplication such as multiple teams assessing the same documents or interviewing the same person.

The auditor should:

- Organize work papers into groups.
- Use checklists to organize information.

A.14 SELECTING SOURCES OF INFORMATION

The auditor can collect, sort, analyze, decipher, gather much data, reports, and information and all manner of sources of information. Auditor may collect the data in a spreadsheet, description of a population of items, electronic media paper media reports, and other forms of information that will have to be sifted to determine if the information is relevant to the scope and specific audit objective.

The auditor should determine what are the critical few pieces of information from the insignificant many. Sources of information may involve the following:

a. **Auditee interviews**
   Aditi interviews.

b. **Auditee observations**
   Walk-around of the auditee's facilities and observations of auditee's work environment and conditions.

c. **Auditee documentation**
   Traditional Management System information such as strategies, plans, policies, procedures, work instructions, and other types of information that may be linked to the audit objective.

d. **Auditee records**
   Meeting records and audit records may be secured such as previous audit reports inspection forms, corrective actions, measurements, tax, and other audit information.

e. **Auditee summaries**
   Key Risk Indicators, Key Performance Indicators, and other measures of performance.

f. Auditee sampling

Records regarding the auditee's inspection, sampling, and measurements.

g. Auditee reports

Auditee reports from external sources, which may include client surveys, measurement data, measurement tool data, statistical analysis, product reviews, and other information.

h. Auditee databases

Electronic media such as spreadsheets, databases, digital reports, statistical analyses, and other forms of electronic media.

i. Auditee simulation

Process and product modeling information.

A.15 VISTING THE AUDITEE'S LOCATION

The auditor may conduct the audit on location specifically at the auditee's facility or may conduct the audit off site. The auditor should not interfere with the auditee's core work processes. The auditor may visit the auditee's process from beginning to end and then interview a supervisor or engineering lead to gather more information.

The auditor at the auditee's location should pay particular attention to:

a. **Audit planning**
   Planning the audit may involve:

   - Obtain approval to visit the auditee's location (s) including determine dates, people to interview, processes to review and information to obtain.
   - Be aware of the auditee's access, health, safety, and environmental requirements. As well, the auditor should be aware of the cultural and ethical requirements of the auditee and obtain the requisite approvals possibly clearances before visiting the facility.
   - Obtain protective equipment and suitable clothing prior to visiting the auditee's facilities.
   - Confirm with the auditee lead on the use of any electronic equipment prior to visiting the auditee's facility. Approval may be required for photography, recording conversations, photo copies of documents, another security and confidential confidentiality Issues.

- Ensure the auditee is aware of all auditing requirements prior to the visit. Except for unannounced audits, sharing information with the auditee is a necessary protocol.

b. Auditee onsite

Audit on-site examinations tips for the audit team:

- Do not interfere with the auditee's core processes.
- Ensure each auditor is properly protected regarding health safety and environmental requirements.
- Understand auditee emergency procedures and communicate these to the audit team.
- Establish communication protocols with the auditee who can address the questions, when are responses expected, what questions can be asked, etc.
- Select audit team members based on the stakeholder requirements, audit objectives, scope and objectives of the audit. The audit team should consider the complexity of the auditee's organization and its processes and products.
- Review with the auditee what is permitted and not permitted during the audit. For example, the audit he may have special equipment, gauges, processes, and products that may not be reviewed.
- Ensure the audit is conducted in a professional manner. The audit team lead should establish protocols with the auditee regarding disagreements, escalation, and resolution of issues.

- Inquire if copies of critical audit information should be secured. Confidential, proprietary, and security documents may not leave a facility or be reproduced.

- Avoid discussing personal information with the auditee. The source of audit information should be identified; however, any personal information cannot be part of the audit papers.

c. **Virtual audit steps**

Virtual audit activities:

- Ensure the audit team understands the protocols for accessing the auditee's Information Technology. This includes access protocols, dual authentication, control of software, etc.

- If the auditor needs to have evidence that is critical to an audit objective, then the auditor should request permission from the auditee to obtain a copy of the information. The requested information may be prior proprietary, confidential, where secured.

- As with on-site audits, the audit team lead should develop understanding protocols, resolution protocols, and escalation protocols with the auditee.

- Identify location of critical data that is used as evidence of compliance to audit objectives.

- Ensure that auditee's confidential and individual information is secured.

- Ensure security and disposition of confidential information and audit evidence. This should be discussed the auditee and communicated to the audit team.

A.16 AUDITING VIRTUAL ACTIVITIES AND LOCATIONS

The audit team may conduct a virtual audit of based on the location of information or the complexity of the organization. Virtual audits are planned, conducted, and reported when the auditee core processes are online, offside, offshore, or otherwise and inaccessible to the auditor. In these cases, the auditee is responsible for identifying these locations and the auditor is responsible for developing an audit plan for conducting virtual audits in different locations.

The audit team lead will still plan, conduct, and report a virtual audit similar to an on-site audit. The audit team lead must obtain evidence to support a finding regarding a specific audit objective even though it is a virtual audit.

The auditor and auditee should ensure that Information Technology and security requirements are communicated and well understood prior to conducting the audit.

The auditor and auditee should address the following:

- Ensure the audit team is following approved auditee protocols, including security, access control, software used, etc.
- Evaluate requirements prior to conducting the audit.
- If there are technical issues or understandings that are unclear, they should be resolved with the auditee. Auditor can develop 'what if' contingency plans.

The auditor should have competence in planning, conducting, and reporting virtual audits. These competencies can include:

- Ability to secure Information Technology and have security protocol knowledge, skills, and abilities regarding access control, electronic commitment, and software security.
- Ability to facilitate meetings so virtual audit can be planned, conducted, and reported adequately.

Just like on-site audits, the audit team lead is responsible for conducting the opening meeting virtually with the auditee. The audit team lead should consider the following:

- Identifying risks and opportunities regarding virtual or remote audits.
- Using schematics, process drawings, floor plans, product diagrams, and other shared information to set a reference for asking specific questions in obtaining evidence.
- Ensuring the electronic connection between the auditor and auditee works and there are no interruptions.
- Ensuring agreement with the auditee for copying, recording, picture taking, and other reproduction about an information, especially regarding confidential, proprietary, and secure documents.
- Ensuring confidentiality of information shared by the auditee as well as ensuring privacy during the virtual meeting.

Commentary: Virtual audits may be the future of Management System auditing. So, it is critical that auditors learn the basics of virtual auditing.

A.17 CONDUCTING INTERVIEWS

The auditor will conduct interviews to obtain and verify critical information while conducting the audit. Interviews are among the most critical means of gathering information regarding a specific requirement or audit objective. The auditor can conduct interviews in person, via telephone, online, or face to face using video.

The auditor should consider the following in conducting interviews regardless of the medium:

a. **Appropriate level interviews**
   Auditee interview is conducted at the appropriate level and appropriate function of the auditee's organization. Interviews may be conducted at the enterprise level, process level, or activity level. The critical item is that the interview can be conducted within scope based on audit objectives.

b. **Interview timing**
   Auditee interviews cannot disrupt auditee core operations. Interviews should be conducted during the auditee's normal working hours and locations.

c. **Auditee comfort**
   Auditor should make the auditee comfortable while conducting the audit and not feel like the auditee is being interrogated.

d. **Reason for interview**
   Purpose, extent, scope, of the interview should be explained to the auditee. As well, any note taking should be explained.

e. **Start of interview**
   Interview can be structured based on the nature and purpose

of the questions. In a structured interview, the auditor may request the authorities and responsibilities of the interviewee.

f. Type of questions

Auditor can ask a number of questions based on the type of interview. In a structured interview, questions regarding and audit objective may be specific, linear, and focused. An unstructured interview, the questions may be open and follow a discussion format.

g. Audit awareness

Interview involves verbal and nonverbal communication even in a virtual setting. Verbal communication is what is said. Nonverbal communication involves facial expressions, body posture, unknown but repetitive habits, and other forms of visual expression that one party communicates to the audit. Again, the purpose of the interview is to obtain objective evidence relating to an audit objective.

h. Interview summary

Auditor or scribe can track and summarize interview notes and observations.

i. Appreciation

After the interview, the auditor should thank the auditee for their assistance and cooperation.

A. 18 AUDIT FINDINGS

A.18.1 Determining Audit Findings

Audit findings are the result of an audit. The auditor will issue of finding based on each audit objective. The auditor should consider the following when issuing a finding:

a. **Audit follow up**
   Explain whether the current audit is new or a follow-up on a previous audit. As well, the auditor can identify previous audit findings and what are the expected results of the new audit.

b. **Audi client requirements**
   Identify who are the audit clients, stakeholders, and interested parties as well as each of their requirements.

c. **Audit accuracy**
   Determine suitability, appropriateness, accuracy, and reliability of the evidence to support each audit objective and its finding.

d. **Audit planning completed**
   Determine how well audit planning, conducting, and reporting is realized against the audit scope, resources, costs and objectives.

e. **Audit findings scope**
   Determine whether the findings meet and satisfy the audit objectives. Findings may state that the objective was met, was not met, and if there are opportunities for improvement.

f. **Audit sampling**
   Depending on the audit objectives regarding a large population of homogeneous items, the auditor may decide to pull a

sample of items from the population. The auditor should define the size of the population, sample size, standard used, and expect an expected competence level.

g. **Group findings**
   Auditor may categorize audit findings as critical, major, or minor or may simply state in a finding that based on observations and evidence the auditee complies with a regulatory standard.

A18.2 Recording Conformities

Auditor for determining compliance with a statutory or regulatory requirement may determine that there is conformity or nonconformity. The auditor to record conformity should consider the following:

a. **Audit criteria description**
   Describe the statutory or regulatory requirements which are the criteria of the audit.

b. **Audit evidence**
   Describe the extent, type, and suitability of the audit evidence to support whether there is conformity to the regulatory requirement.

c. **Auditor declaration**
   Declare conformity if appropriate.

18.3 RECORDING NON-CONFORMITIES

Auditor may determine the auditee does not conform to the specific regulatory requirement or audit objective. In these cases, the auditor should consider the following:

a. **Audit criteria description**
   Describe the statutory regulatory audit criteria.

b. **Audit evidence**
   State extent, type, and suitability of the audit evidence to support weather the audit conforms to the regulatory requirement.

c. **Auditor declaration**
   Declare that there is nonconformity.

d. **Audit related findings**
   State what type of follow-up is required as a result of the nonconformity whether it is appropriate to the scope of the audit.

A.18.4 DEALING WITH FINDINGS RELATED TO MULTIPLE CRITERIA

The auditor may encounter multiple criteria in an audit objective. In these cases, the auditor may issue multiple findings. Or in reviewing multiple Management Systems, the auditor may issue one finding to multiple Management Systems. The auditor should consider the impacts and risks all Management Systems being audited.

Auditor should consider and discuss the following with the audit client:

a. **Criteria findings**
   Develop separate findings for each audit criterion and audit objective.

b. **Single finding**
   Develop a single finding to multiple audit criteria.

The auditor should discuss theses with the audit client and develop an appropriate response in terms of providing support and guidance to the auditee on how to respond to these findings.

RISK GLOSSARY

4P's: Trademarked business risk model representing: Proactive, Preventive, Predictive, Preemptive™ actions focused around risk management.

Accidental hazard: Source of harm or hazard created by error, negligence, or unintentional failure.

Adaptive leadership: Is a practical leadership and management framework to address, adapt, and thrive in today is VUCA (Volatility, Uncertainty, Complexity, and Ambiguity) business environment. Adaptive leadership is based on flexibility and risk management.

Annex SL: High level structure, provides identical core text, and provides key definitions that will be found in future and revised Management System standards.

Annual Risk Report: Document compiled by the Risk Board with consolidated ISO 31000 ERM analysis, risk reports, and treatment plans.

Application controls: Application controls refer to transaction processing controls, sometimes called 'input - processing - output' controls in an IT environment.

Assessment risk: Risk the organization did not identify, monitor, or root cause eliminate.

Audit report: Independent review of operations and/or finance for adherence to standards.

Auditability: Ease, consistency, and accuracy of auditing to ISO 9001:2015 or audit Management System requirements.

Baldrige: Stands for Malcolm Baldrige National Quality Award.

Black Swan: Event that is high consequence and low likelihood.

Board of Directors Audit Committee: Board responsible for reviewing Internal Control over Financial Reporting and operational risks.

Bowtie Method: Risk assessment visual method for looking at potential causes of failure or risk and developing plausible scenario. The reason it is called a bowtie is because the diagrams look like a bow where the causes are on the left side and the consequences are on right side.

Brainstorming: Risk assessment and group problem solving technique to increase the quantity, quality, and diversity of creative ideas.

Business assurance: New offering by Certification Bodies to provide higher levels of assurance beyond ISO conformance.

Business case: Rationale for a new project or process.

Business impact analysis: Systematic approach to look at the potential consequences of an interruption in a critical process, business project, disaster, or accident.

Business Management System: Set of interrelated generic processes within an organization that focuses on meeting business objectives.

Cause and Consequence Analysis: Risk assessment technique for assessing a chain of consequences. The purpose of the risk assessment is to recognize a series of consequences that originate from a failure, hazard, risk or unexpected events.

Cause and Effect Analysis: Risk assessment technique to analyze the causes of an activity or failure. Cause and effect is called an Ishikawa or fish bone diagram.

CRO: Acronym for Chief Risk Officer.

Certification Body: independent company that audits and assures an ISO Quality Management System adheres to specific requirements of the ISO 9001:2015 standard.

CERM: Acronym for Certified Enterprise Risk Manager® certificate.

Checklist: Consists of a series of critical questions (often yes/no) to consider in a risk assessment, process, or activity. Checklist ensures that most critical issues are addressed.

Communication: Process of sharing and obtaining risk information with stakeholders. Information relates to the existence, extent, management, control, and assurance of risk.

Competence: Ability to apply knowledge, ability, and skills to conduct the work required.

Competency framework: Model for new quality organization. Expression was coined by UK Chartered Quality Institute.

Conformity: referred as a conformance. Binary decision (yes/no) to determine adherence to requirements.

Control: Strategy, tactic, or activity that is modifying a risk.

Core functions: Central services and processes of the organization.

Consequence: Outcome of an event that can impact business or audit objectives. Event can lead to range of circumstances. Circumstance can be certain or uncertain and can have positive or negative effects.

Consequence rating: Critical rating element and vector of risk along with 'risk consequence'; risk likelihood starts at a 1 rating, which is insignificant to a 5 rating, which is catastrophic.

Context: Environment in which the organization operates and achieves its business objectives.

Continual improvement: Process of surpassing business objectives.

Control: Modifying or changing risk. Controls can be process, policy, device, practice, procedure, or guideline to modify risk. Control may not result in modifying the effect. Often referred to risk control.

Control environment: Includes: culture, governance, risk management, values, operating style, ethics, and ethos. Sometimes, the control environment is distilled into the expression 'Tone at the Top'.

Control materiality: Reference point to categorize the magnitude of an impact or consequence.

Control owner: Person or function responsible for managing risk and developing the risk policy, procedure, or work instruction.

Controlled risk: Level of risk taking into account the controls in place.

Corporate knowledge: History of risks provide insight into future threats or opportunities.

COSO: Acronym for Committee of Sponsoring Organizations of the Treadway Commission. COSO is a joint initiative of financial organizations to provide guidance on ERM, GRC, ethics, and financial reporting.

COSO ERM: Risk management framework consisting of eight elements: 1. Internal environment; 2. Objective setting; 3. Event identification; 4. Risk assessment; 5. Risk response; 6. Control activities; 7. Information communication; 8. Monitoring.

Correction: Process or action to detect and eliminate nonconformance.

CQO: Acronym for Chief Quality Officer.

CSR: Acronym for Corporate Social Responsibility based on ISO 26000 standards.

Customer: Person(s) who receives a product or service through a value exchange.

Decision Tree Analysis: Risk assessment graphical technique to review decision flow in a tree diagram.

Decision traps: Barriers to RBT, Risk Based Problem Solving and Risk Based Decision Making.

Delphi Method: Structured risk assessment and forecasting technique that relies on a panel of knowledge domain experts to frame and solve a problem.

DIS: Acronym for Draft International Standard.

Disruptive innovation: Innovation that helps create a new market and value that eventually disrupts an existing market and value network.

Documented information: Controlled information to document a QMS or audit Management System.

Downside risk: Risk associated with negative consequences.

Due diligence: Effort a party makes to avoid harm to any audit party.

Due care: Care that a reasonable person would exercise under the circumstances; the standard for determining legal duty.

Due professional care: Application of auditing diligence and judgment.

Enhanced Risk Management: Equivalent Enterprise Risk Management term used in ISO 31000.

Economic Consequence: Effect of an occurrence or event on the value of property, process, or facility.

Enterprise Risk Management (COSO): Integrated COSO framework published in 2004 defines ERM as a "process, affected by an entity is Board of Directors, management and audit personnel, applied in a strategy setting and across the enterprise, designed to identify potential events that may affect the entity, and manage risk to be within its risk appetite, to provide reasonable assurance regarding the achievement of entity objectives." Comprehensive risk program designed to continuously identify and manage real and potential threats, hazards, and opportunities in the organization. Comprehensive and entity level approach to risk management that engages systems, processes, and activities to improve the quality of Risk Based Problem Solving and Risk Based Decision Making to foster the organization is ability to reach its strategic objectives.

Environmental Risk Assessment: Proactive and systematic process for anticipating and protecting risks to human health, welfare, safety, and environment.

Effectiveness: Ability to meet a desired result or business result.

Efficiency: Being able to meet a desired result using optimized resources.

Emerging risk: Evolving or new risk that is difficult to control or manage since its likelihood, consequence, timing, dependencies, interdependencies, and timing are highly uncertain.

ERM control cycle: Continuing and systematic cycle by which risk is identified; evaluated; risk appetite is determined; risk limits are set; risk is treated; risk is monitored; and risk is assured. Control cycle is often based on a risk management framework cycle.

ERM heavy: Refers to COSO risk management framework.

ERM light: Refers to ISO 31000 risk management framework.

ERM risk map: Graphical representation or roll up of risks for the organization considering current level of controls.

Establishing the context: Internal and external boundary conditions and scope related to managing risk, setting criteria, and defining risk management policy. Definition of the external and internal parameters and conditions to be considered when managing risks. Setting up the risk criteria for the risk management policy.

Event: Occurrence or change in a set of circumstances. Event can have one or more causes. Event is called an incident or accident. Event with no consequences is called an incident or near miss. Incident and situation that occurs at a specific place during a specific time.

Event tree: Graphical risk assessment used to illustrate the range of probabilities of possible outcomes that can arise from an initiating event.

Event Tree Analysis: Forward looking, bottom up risk assessment technique that evaluates possible risks. Event tree analyzes the effects of an operating system given that an event has occurred.

Evidence based approach: Rational method for reaching reliable and reproducible audit conclusions and findings.

Executive management: Senior organizational management that establishes and review organizational strategic direction; develops strategic risk plan; develops Key Performance Indicators (KPI is) and Key Risk Indicators (KRI is); establishes and embeds risk management culture; oversees risk management; and reviews and approves risk controls and treatment.

Exposure: Extent to which an organization is exposed to an event.

External context: External environment in which the enterprise operates and establishes its business objectives. External context can include: culture, social, political, legal, regulatory, financial, technological, economic, natural, and competitive criteria.

Failure Modes and Effects Analysis: Systematic approach for identifying possible failures modes, which audit ways a product or process may fail. Failure may mean nonconforming products, errors, software defects, or processes not meeting specifications.

Fault tree: Graphic risk assessment tool used to illustrate the range, probability, and interaction of causal occurrences or events that can lead to a final outcome.

Fault Tree Analysis: Used in safety and reliability problem solving. Fault tree analysis includes deductive problem solving to understand the consequences of an event.
Fault tree analysis model works backward to understand and deduce what causes and event.

FMEA: Acronym for Failure Mode Effects Analysis.

GAGAS: Acronym for Generally Accepted Government Auditing Standards; professional standards presented in the 2011 revision of Government Auditing Standards provide a framework for performing high quality audits.

General controls: IT controls often described in two categories: IT general controls (ITGC) and IT application controls; used in IT environment; controls, audit than application controls, which relate to the environment within which computer based application systems are developed, maintained and operated, and which is therefor applicable to all applications.

Governance: Process by which the Board of Directors reviews the decisions and actions of executive management.

Governance control: a Board level control, which includes oversight, monitoring, and determination of risk appetite.

Governance Risk Compliance (GRC): Governance, risk management, and compliance or GRC is the umbrella term covering an organization is approach across areas; while interpreted differently in various organizations. GRC typically encompasses activities such as corporate governance, ERM, and corporate compliance with applicable laws and regulations.

Guide: Facilitator chosen by the auditee to support the audit team.

Guide 73: Common risk management definitions that will be incorporated into each Management System using RBT.

Hazard: Man made source or cause of difficulty or harm, which may be intentional or unintentional.

Hazard Analysis and Critical Control Points (HACCP): Risk assessment approach to assess hazards in manufacturing, food safety, and audit production processes. Purpose is to identify hazards occurring in the process and to evaluate control effectiveness at critical control points.

Hazard and Operability Analysis (HAZOP): HAZOP analysis evaluates safety, operating, maintenance, and design risks.

Human Reliability Analysis: Risk assessment technique and study of human factors and human performance used in military, medicine, and manufacturing.

IIA: Acronym for Institute for Internal Auditing.

Impact: Same as consequence. Estimated result including financial and operational that would be realized if a risk event would occur.

Independence: Independence from parties whose risks might be harmed by the results of an audit; specific internal management issues are inadequate risk management, inadequate internal controls, and poor governance.

Inherent risk: Risk that the account, disclosure, or financial statement being attested to by an independent firm is materially misstated without considering internal controls, error, or fraud.

Integrated Management System: Single Management System that integrates elements of multiple Management Systems.

Integrity: Basis of professionalism. Includes elements of honesty, diligence, responsibility, and honesty.

Intentional hazard: Source of harm or difficulty created by planned course of action.

Interested parties: Person or organization that can impact or be impacted by a decision. Common interested parties may include stakeholders, clients, owners, employees, suppliers, NGOs, regulators, etc.

Internal context: Internal environment in which the enterprise operates and establishes its business objectives. Internal context can include: governance, organizational structure, roles, accountabilities, policies, procedures, strategies, plans, tactics, capabilities, resources, perceptions, values, stakeholders, IT, relationships, standards, specifications, contracts, and culture.

Internal control: Integral component of an organization is management that provides reasonable assurance that the following objectives are being achieved: effectiveness and efficiency of operations, reliability of financial reporting, and compliance with applicable laws and regulations.

Internal review: Review undertaken to assess the suitability, adequacy, effectiveness, and efficiency of operational systems and to determine opportunities for improvement.

Intervention risk: Risk the organization did not treat and correct the problem at the symptom and root cause levels.

Issues log: Record of issues faced and actions taken to remediate them. Issues identified as risks are assessed and treated.

ISO: Acronym for International Organization of Standardization.

ISO 9001:2015: ISO Quality Management System standard, which was finalized in Q3 of 2015.

ISO 19011: Comprehensive standard for conducting Management System certification audits.

ISO 31000: Risk management framework or guideline used as reference for many ISO families of standards.

Key Performance Indicator (KPI): Measure(s) on the achievement toward a control objective.

KRI: Acronym for Key Risk Indicator. Measure(s) that can provide an early warning that a risk has occurred or is recurring.

Layer of Protection Analysis: Risk assessment technique is a process risk assessment and hazard tool, which looks at potential hazardous events, their consequences, initiating causes, and likelihoods of occurring.

Level of risk: Magnitude of risk. Expressed in terms of likelihood and consequence.

Likelihood: Possibility or chance of something occurring or happening. Likelihood is called probability or frequency.

Management control: Controlling is one of the managerial functions like planning, organizing, staffing and directing; important function because it helps to check the errors and to take the corrective action so that deviation from standards are minimized and stated goals are achieved in a desired manner. How well the organization is identifying, controlling, and mitigating risk.

Management System: Interrelated processes within an organization whose aim is to achieve business objectives.

Markov Analysis: Risk assessment method to evaluate the relative reliability of system components. Can be used to determine dependencies between components, personnel, and technologies.

Materiality: Concept in accounting and auditing relating to the importance or significance of an amount, transaction, finding, or discrepancy.

Materiality levels: Thresholds the organization uses to determine risks at the enterprise and entity level.

Measurement: Process to determine a value or number.

Mitigation plan: Strategy for risk mitigation. If an identified risk is not within the risk appetite, risk tolerance, or risk retention, then further mitigation is planned.

Monitoring: Continual checking, observing, and supervising the status of risk to determine changes that may affect controls or residual risk.

Monte Carlo Method: Risk assessment method for analyzing engineering and physical phenomena. Monte Carlo methods are used for optimization. Monte Carlo method can be used with a probabilistic distribution so information can be inferred from a large population of data.

Natural hazard: Source of harm created by environmental phenomena.

Non conformity: referred as a nonconformance. Binary decision (yes/no) to determine adherence to requirements. In this case, an inability to conform to requirements.

Objective: Result to be gained or achieved.

Observer: Person who accompanies the audit team and ensures that procedures are consistently followed.

Operational risk: Potential of loss attributable to process variation or disruption in operations caused by internal or external factors.

Opportunity: Chance for an advancement, improvement, or progress.

Organization: Legal entity that has processes and functions that achieve business objectives.

Outsource: External organization providing products or services.

PDCA: Acronym for Plan - Do - Check - Act.

PESTLE: Acronym for Political, Economic, Sociological, Technical, Legal, and Environmental. Commonly used as a planning tool to identify and prioritize threats in the external environment.

People risk: People audit backbone and personality of a business; people are a key source of risk, because risk management is the fundamental driver to sustainable success, understanding the various risks associated with employees that must be a top priority for business leaders and policymakers.

Performance: Actionable or measurable output or outcome.

Preliminary Hazard Analysis: Preliminary hazard analysis is the review of potential threats, events, or risks. Hazard is a potential condition that may exist or not occur. Hazard may not be anticipated or planned. Hazard may be unknown or even unknowable due to a potential 'black swan', cascading risk, or interactive risk factors.

Preventive action: Change implemented to address a weakness in a Management System that is not yet responsible for causing nonconforming product or service.

Priority risk: Risks that are still high after risk controls and treatment.

Probability: Measure of the change of occurrence, a number between 0 and 1 where 1 is absolute certainty.

Process: Interrelated and/or interacting activities that add value to inputs to create an output.

Process analysis: Approach to evaluate operational and service performance and identify opportunities for improvement.

Process risk: Probability of loss inherent in a business process; may include lack of process capability, lack of process stability, and/or lack of improvement.

Professional judgment: Standard of care that requires auditors to exercise reasonable care and diligence and to observe the principles of serving the public interest and maintaining the highest degree of integrity, objectivity, and independence in applying professional judgment to all aspects of their work.

Project risk: Project risk involves not being able to meet project objectives or deliverables based on project scope, quality, schedule, or cost.

Quality assurance: Engineering activities implemented in a quality system so product or service requirements can be fulfilled.

Quality management: Management of quality related activities, including assurance and control.

Quality Management Thinking (QMT): Quality equivalent to Risk Based Thinking (RBT).

Quality governance: Process by which the Board of Directors reviews RBT, quality decisions and actions of executive management.

QMS: Acronym for Quality Management System.

RBT: Acronym for ISO Risk Based Thinking. First stage in a RCMM journey from RBT to risk assessment, risk management, to ISO 31000 ERM.

RCMM: Acronym for Risk Capability Maturity Model, which consists of five levels from ad hoc to optimized.

Reasonable assurance: Most cost effective measures are taken in the design and implementation stages to reduce risk and restrict expected deviations to a tolerable level.

Red Book: Institute of Internal Auditors (IIA) guidelines for conducting an internal audit.

Reliability Centered Analysis: Risk assessment analysis focuses on long term quality and lifecycle management of a product. Can be used in reliability centered maintenance, product failure, or operational safety analysis.

Reputational risk: Decrease in brand equity or credibility in the organization.

Requirement: Explicit or implicit needs or expectations. Customers, regulators, or interested parties can develop a requirement.

Residual risk. Risk remaining after risk treatment. Residual risk can contain unidentified risk. Residual risk is called retained risk. Exposure to loss remaining after audit known risks have been countered, factored in, or eliminated.

Review: Activity used to determine the suitability, adequacy, and effectiveness of risk controls against established objectives.

Risk: Uncertainty on achieving a business objective. Risk is a deviation from an objective, which can be either positive or negative. Objectives can be from the financial, quality, project, process, program, transactional, or supply chain. Qualitative risk is defined as likelihood and consequence. Potential that a chosen action or activity (including the choice of inaction) will lead to a loss (an undesirable outcome). Qualitative risk is defined as the consequence and likelihood of an event. Potential event with a negative or undesirable outcome, which may include the potential failure to capitalize on an opportunity.

Risk analysis: Process to understand the nature of risk and to determine the level of risk. Risk analysis is the basis for risk evaluation and decisions about risk treatment and risk management.

Risk acceptance: Explicit or implicit risk based decision to take no action that would impact or affect all or part of a specific risk.

Risk aggregation: Collection of risk (categories and impact) to develop an understanding of the overall risk to the enterprise.

Risk analysis: Systematic examination of risk components and characteristics.

Risk appetite: Level of risk that an organization is prepared to accept, before action is deemed necessary to reduce it; sometimes called 'risk tolerance.' Amount and type of strategic risk the organization is willing to pursue and manage.

Risk assessment: Process of identifying, analyzing, and evaluating risk. Determination of quantitative or qualitative value of risk related to a concrete situation and a recognized threat (called hazard).

Risk assurance: Ability to provide requisite level of risk control effectiveness and competence of effectiveness controls.

Risk attitude: Organization is approach to assess and mitigate risk. Risk management is an element of risk attitude.

Risk aversion: Attitude and policy to move away and not pursue opportunities and actions.

Risk avoidance: Risk Based Decision Making to be not involved in an activity or to withdraw from an activity in order not to be exposed to a specific risk.

Risk Based Auditing: known as Value Added Auditing. Red Book and Yellow Book are examples of Risk Based Auditing.

Risk Based Certification: DNV term for high level, risk certification and assurance.

Risk Based Decision Making. Critical element of ISO Risk Based Thinking (RBT).

Risk Based Problem Solving. Critical element of ISO Risk Based Thinking (RBT).

Risk Based Thinking (RBT): International Organization for Standardization (ISO) tagline for ISO 9001:2015 and possibly families of standards as it incorporates risk. ISO says that RBT has always been part of ISO standards. RBT is defined in this book as: 1. Risk Based Problem Solving and 2. Risk Based Decision Making.

Risk Based Thinking journey: Steps in risk journey from RBT to risk assessment, risk management, to ISO 31000 ERM.

Risk Capability Maturity Model (RCMM): Methodology used to define and identify an organization is risk control processes, procedures, and protocols. Model is often based in terms on a five level evolutionary scale from ad hoc to world class, risk management.

Risk category: Distinct classes of risk, where similar opportunities and risks can be analyzed and compared.

Risk control: Method by which firms evaluate potential losses and take action to reduce or eliminate such threats. Risk control is a technique that utilizes findings from risk assessments (identifying potential risk factors in a firm is operations).

Risk criteria: Terms against which risk is evaluated. Risk criteria are based on business objectives, external/internal context, and audit criteria. Risk criteria can be based on standards, laws, policies, and audit requirements.

Risk description: Structured statement of risk containing five elements: source of risk, events, causes, consequences, and likelihood.

Risk escalation: Communication of risks to the appropriate level of management requiring additional resources for treatment.

Risk evaluation: Process of comparing the results of risk analysis against risk criteria to determine whether it is acceptable or tolerable to the enterprise. Risk evaluation is used in the decision of risk treatment. Assessing probability and impact of individual risks taking into account any interdependencies or audit factors outside the immediate scope under investigation.

Risk event: Occurrence or change in a particular set of circumstances that have negative consequences.

Risk governance: Processes to ensure authorities and accountabilities for managing enterprise risk, deploying risk management framework, implementing risk management process, and proving risk assurance is appropriate to the organization.

Risk identification: Process of finding, recognizing, and describing risk. Risk identification involves identifying risk sources, events, likelihood, and possible consequences. Risk identification involves historical data, theoretical analysis, expert opinions, and stakeholder needs.

Risk inventory: List of prioritized organizational risks.

Risk level: Nature and threshold for risk based on likelihood and consequence assessment.

Risk likelihood rating: Critical rating element and vector of risk along with 'risk consequence'; risk likelihood starts at a 1 rating, which is a rare event to a 5 rating, which is almost certain.

Risk limit: Threshold used to monitor actual risk exposure of a unit or units of an organization to ensure the level of aggregate risk remains within the risk appetite or risk tolerance.

Risk management: Identification, assessment, and prioritization of risks (effect of uncertainty on objectives, whether positive or negative) followed by effective and economic application of resources to minimize, monitor, control, and assure the probability and/or consequence of negative events or to maximize opportunities.

Risk management framework: Process cycle for managing risk. ISO 31000 and COSO are two common risk management frameworks.

Risk management plan: Steps, procedures, approach, resources, methodology, and components applied to the management of upside and downside risk.

Risk management: Also, called risk mitigation or risk control. Risk management is defined as the control of risk.

Risk management framework: Structure on which to build strategy or set of controls organized in categories to be able to reach objectives, monitor, and assure performance.

Risk management policy: Policy is the highest level documentation and organizational direction relating to risk management.

Risk management process: Systematic application of organizational policies, procedures, work instructions, processes, protocols, practices, and guidelines for establishing the context, analyzing, assessing, treating, monitoring and communicating risks.

Risk map: Visual method of laying out the risk of an event or variation; visual representation of statistics; consisting of red, yellow, and green elements.

Risk Management System: Similar to ISO Management Systems, such as Quality Management System (QMS) and Environmental Management System (EMS). ISO 31000 can form the basis for a risk Management System.

Risk matrix: Risk assessment tool for ranking and illustrating components of risk in an array.

Risk metric: Measure of risk. Can include Key Risk Indicators, value at risk, or tail exposures, Cpk, etc.

Risk mitigation: System, process, or investment to control the likelihood or consequence of a risk.

Risk monitoring: Last major element of ISO 31000 risk management process, used to determine if risk management plan is being followed and if internal risk controls are working effectively.

Risk owner: Enterprise owner with the accountability, authority, and responsibility to manage risk. Additional responsibilities include: identify risks in span of control; ensure risks with control area are managed appropriately; develop treatment plans; monitor risk control and treatment; ensure treatment owners are assigned; place risks on enterprise register; and escalate risks if necessary.

Risk profile: Description of the set of risks that can relate to the enterprise. Comprehensive view of risk the organization faces.

Risk reduction: called risk control.

Risk register: Record of risk information by level and type of risk.

Risk reporting: Form of risk communication intended to inform stakeholders, clients, or interested parties' current state of risk and its treatment.

Risk response: Used similarly as risk treatment or risk mitigation; appropriate steps taken or procedures implemented on discovery of an unacceptably high degree of exposure to one or more risks.

Risk retention: If a risk is within the organizational risk appetite, then the risk is accepted; no additional controls are required, but are continuously monitored for suitability.

Risk sharing: Form of Risk Based Decision Making involving the agreed on distribution of risk among parties.

Risk source: Element(s) that have the potential that can cause risk.

Risk syntax: Use and application of risk concepts. See 'risk taxonomy.'

Risk taxonomy: Practice and science of risk classification of things or concepts and principles that underlie the classification.

Risk tolerance: Acceptable level of variation a company or an individual is willing to accept in the pursuit of the specific objective. Aggregate risk taking capacity of the enterprise.

Risk transfer: Form of Risk Based Decision Making to manage risk so that it shifts some or all of the risk to an audit party, system, process, geography, supplier, or network.

Risk treatment: Process of managing risk, including: searching for opportunities; avoiding risk; increasing risk; removing the risk source; changing likelihood; changing consequences; sharing the risk; or retaining the risk. Risk treatment is called risk elimination, risk prevention, risk reduction, risk response, or risk management.

Root cause analysis: Risk Based Problem Solving method to identify the primary cause of a recurring, chronic, or systemic problem.

Scenario analysis: Risk assessment process to identify, assess, and evaluate possible outcomes based on specific assumptions. Outcomes are potential and realizable projections or alternatives of the future.

Scenario test: Process for assessing the adverse consequences of one or more possible events occurring simultaneously or serially.

SMART objectives: Acronym representing: Specific, Measurable, Assignable, Realistic, and Timely

Sneak circuit analysis: Risk assessment method to determine safety of mission critical electronic and mechanical components.

Self-certification: Statement by an organization that it meets ISO requirements without a third-party, certification audit.

Speed of onset: Time it takes for a risk event to occur or manifest.

Stakeholder: Enterprise or person that can impact or be impacted by risk.

Stakeholder analysis: Process identifying individuals who have a vested interest in achieving business objectives and uncertainties.

Stress test: Process for measuring the adverse consequence on one or more quality, supplier, ISO, design, cyber security, Information Technology, people, or audit operational factors that can impact the organization is financial profile.

Structured interview: Follows a standardized checklist or procedure to conduct a series of interviews. Structured interview is used as part of audit types of quantitative or qualitative risk assessments or survey research to scope or frame a problem.

Structured 'What IF' Technique: Called SWIFT technique. Swift is a high to low risk assessment technique that is often used with audit risk assessment tools such as Failure Mode and Effects Analysis and brainstorming.

Supplier: Organization or person providing a product or service as part of a value exchange.

Survey: Gather data on risk, threats, and hazards.

SWOT: Acronym for Strengths - Weaknesses - Opportunities - Threats. Commonly used as a planning tool for assessing risk and evaluating a business.

System: Set of interrelated and interacting activities.

Technical Committee (TC) 176: ISO committee responsible for writing QMS standard, ISO 9001:2015.

Technical controls: Example of control with IT and ICS systems; control consists of identification and authentication.

Technical expert: Person with specific knowledge who is part of the audit team.

Technology risk: Risk that key technology processes a company uses to develop, deliver, and manage its products, services, and support operations do not meet requirements.

Threat: Natural or man-made activity with the potential to cause damage, injury, or loss.

Top management: Same as executive management. Group that controls an organization at the highest level.

TQM: Acronym for Total Quality Management. Implies a high level of quality maturity and capability.

Treatment owner: Person responsible for treating the risk.

Upside risk: Opportunity or positive risk.

VUCA: Acronym for Volatility, Uncertainty, Complexity, and Ambiguity. Description of current business environment that requires different strategic and tactical planning models.

Vulnerability: Susceptibility of the enterprise to a risk event related to the entity is preparedness, agility, and adaptability.

White space risk: Risks in the white spaces between silos, functions, and work between processes.

Yellow Book: called GAGAS or Generally Accepted Government Auditing Standards. Audit standards for public auditing in U.S. and Canada.

Index

B

C

S

44856201R00115

Made in the USA
San Bernardino, CA
23 July 2019